Praise for

"The rising popularity of yoga in the US has, unfortunately, been focused on the physical benefits of the longstanding traditions of movements and positions. While yoga can bring improvements in physical strength and flexibility, we have lost the true essence of the practice, which is to initiate a conversation and facilitate growth of the connections among body, mind, and spirit.

"In *The Path of Joyful Living*, Dani McGuire presents a brave and transparent testimony of the internal dialogue that is an inherent part of being human. Through the lens of yoga's traditions and practices, she gives the reader a roadmap for honest, thought-provoking self-dialogue. Whether used as part of a yoga practice or as a guide for meditation, *The Path of Joyful Living* is a provocative yet gentle mirror that will stimulate, inspire, and push readers to the next level of their personal best."

– Angela LaSalle, MD, DABFM, ABOIM, medical director integrative medicine, Parkview Health System, Fort Wayne

"In this succinct and bold book, Dani McGuire is raw, revealing, and passionate. She draws from many wells of truth as she languages the 'I am love' story in a personal and transformative way. This book is sure to inspire both seasoned mindful meditators and those who are new to the way of self-compassion and joyful living."

– Dave Johnson, PhD, RN, LMFT, mental health and mindfulness educator, professor of nursing at University of Saint Francis, Fort Wayne

"Dani McGuire's approach strikes a 'human' balance between a most beautiful and articulate expression of ancient teachings and her background as an entrepreneur and mother of two who has a wicked sense of humor. She is pure authenticity, and that shines in her writing, teaching, and presence."

– David Romanelli, health and wellness innovator, author of *Life Lessons from the Oldest and Wisest*

The Path *of* Joyful Living

The Path of Joyful Living
CULTIVATING MINDFUL ACTION THROUGH YOGA

DANI MCGUIRE

Balance. Harmony. Flow.

Sattva Vinyasa Press
Fort Wayne, Indiana

Published by Sattva Vinyasa Press
www.sattvavinyasa.com

© 2018 by Dani McGuire
All rights reserved under International and Pan American copyright conventions. No part of this book may be reproduced or utilized in any form, by electronic, mechanical, or other means, without the prior written permission of the publisher, except for brief quotations embodied in literary articles or reviews.

Sattva Vinyasa™ is a registered trademark of Danielle M. McGuire.

Cover and interior design by Katie Brown
Cover photo by Scott Foltz
Author photo by Tim Brumbeloe

ISBN 978-1-7327498-0-1 (paperback)

Manufactured in the United States of America
10 9 8 7 6 5 4 3 2 1

This book is dedicated to seekers of truth—
to those who are curious about yoga, relationship,
and living an authentic life of meaning, inspiration,
and service.
Join me on the path to Joy.

CONTENTS

Foreword by Shiva Rea .... *xi*

Preface .... *xv*

Setting an Intention for Reading .... *xix*

    Introduction 1

    Step 1: Awareness 13

    Step 2: Embodiment 39

    Step 3: Surrender 113

    The Fourth Phase: Integration 139

Acknowledgments *145*

Notes *147*

FOREWORD BY SHIVA REA

In your hands you hold a treasure. *The Path of Joyful Living* is the life work of beloved yoga teacher Dani McGuire. While most new and long-time yoga practitioners are aware of the ubiquitous eight limbs of yoga, the three-part process of *kriya yoga*, the "yoga of action," is less known. As a contemporary exploration of kriya yoga, this book offers the wisdom of Patanjali's Yoga Sutras from the perspective of a skilled yoga therapist dedicated to the transformation of suffering into freedom.

Dani asks us: "In every moment, we can put one of two messages out into the world: either 'I need love' or 'I am love.' If you pause to notice your thoughts and actions, you can most often trace them back to one of these two seed thoughts." This is one of the most insightful and practical entryways into the wisdom of the Yoga Sutras I have ever encountered. As we pause, we can feel the shift of consciousness at a cellular level from grasping and separation, which Dani describes as emerging from disconnection from the source within, to a deeper connection with that source—the ability of the "self to dwell in its own nature," *tada drashtuh svarupe avasthanam* (Yoga Sutra 1.3).

Dani offers compassion and skillfulness honed from her years of holding space for the deeper, fundamental cause of suffering that kriya yoga addresses—the split from the ground of being. She emphasizes the need to heal the deeper splits within ourselves. Then she takes her readers on a journey toward embodied integration of self-love through practical meditations, life-changing inquiries, and wisdom teachings. Dani's vulnerability in sharing her early experiences with anxiety, depression, and eating disorders as well as everyday life challenges is what is missing from most explorations of the Yoga Sutras.

I celebrate the beauty of Dani's own integrated embodiment informed by many teachers and paths. Dani is a gifted graduate of the Prana Vinyasa Global School for Living Yoga program. The flowering of her own path and the founding of Sattva Vinyasa Yoga and Pranayoga Institute is an expression of the empowerment that has come from her own cellular fertilization. Her integration of ayurveda, somatics, and yoga therapy into a flowing, living vinyasa is a great contribution to the world.

Dani is a beautiful mover, but she has chosen to make her first book offering about the movement of consciousness that is awakened through the yoga of action, devotion, and service. At a time when the Western yoga world is being visually bombarded by advanced yoga asanas flooding social media, Dani offers a refreshing counterpoint, taking the reader on a deeper soul-journey. Deeper backbends don't always lead to a more open heart, just as accomplishment in arm balances doesn't always mean greater balance in life. Dani courageously brings her yoga therapy wisdom as an offering to the world's body-mind split, stressors, and suffering.

Yoga Sutra 2.16 says: *heyam duhkham anagatam*, "Avoidable is the suffering that has not come." As an antidote to the suffering that can be addressed and liberated, *The Path of Joyful Living* is a book to keep by your side to imbibe. It truly illuminates kriya yoga and the eight limbs of yoga for healing in everyday life. As we begin to shift from the underlying triggers through cultivating the meditations in this book, a natural flow of consciousness, a joy of embodied being, begins to permeate our life. We discover being present even as we are pulled by the tides of life's ups and downs, being Love as the emanation of our very nature, being Yoga as the essence of meditation.

May all beings be happy and free,
And may the thoughts, words, and actions of my own life
contribute to that happiness and freedom for all.

Be prepared to be changed as you move through this book, for you will not be the same person you were before you began reading.

PREFACE

This book has grown out of my two decades of studying and teaching yoga and yoga therapy, and offering yoga therapy and Ayurveda consultations. A lot of this work has been about holding space for others to face the suffering that is part of our human condition and to uncover the core of contentment at their center. This is what I was unknowingly seeking myself when I began my own yoga practice. I was nineteen and facing treatments with antidepressants and anxiety medication to manage a full-blown eating disorder along with panic attacks and thoughts of suicide. As I became aware of the people-pleasing, type A mental disorder that was the root of my symptoms, I was able to step outside myself enough to look elsewhere for a solution. Searching for "something natural," I decided to try yoga.

The first moments of my very first yoga class felt like magic. The practice of the postures was so different from the overadrenalized workouts I was used to. Now, after years of study and training, including working for a neurosurgeon as a yoga therapist and training yoga teachers and yoga therapists, I know that magical feeling was the firing up of my parasympathetic nervous system, something that I had previously accessed only after vomiting or sex or imbibing some substance or achieving something on my insane to-do list. However, unlike the follow-up to those behaviors, after yoga I didn't feel like a failure or that I needed the next fix. Instead, I realized that I was okay. I would discover later that realizing we are okay and provided for is a step toward realizing that our essence is Love.

As I studied more yoga and became trained as a yoga teacher, I began to dive into the philosophy supporting yoga, the eightfold path laid out in Patanjali's Yoga Sutras and especially the Bhagavad Gita. And through my yoga practice, I was able to slow down enough to arrive in the present moment. Grounded in the present, I could then begin to notice the negative mental chatter and emotional emptiness inside me. Not turning away from the chatter and emptiness, but instead becoming curious about them, was enough to begin the transformation from experiencing more suffering to experiencing more ease. I began to heal at all levels—mental and emotional and also physical. Over time, I became more than okay. I became a leader, helping others to find their way out of their own dark places.

I was not a writer before writing this book. I wrote blogs now and then, but the idea of writing a book was never on the horizon. Still, something kept tugging at my heart, telling me to put my thoughts, feelings, and experiences on paper for others to read. I have felt an overwhelming love for the students and care-seekers I have worked with, and this book is partially a song to them. They have been open to transforming their own suffering into ease by using the tools of the yoga lineages and yoga therapies that have been passed through me to them; they have been my teachers as I have learned and grown as a yoga therapist and Ayurveda wellness counselor. It has been a blessing to witness them discovering that they are more than okay—they are whole.

My hope is that, as you read this book, you will discover that you are whole. This book is meant to be more than another "self-help" book. It is designed to move you through a process of self-discovery—of remembering who you are, how you can serve, and how much you are loved. I hope that as you discover this for yourself, you will pass on the message of love in the unique way that only you can, in your household and community, and to your students if you are a yoga teacher. Love is a door that leads us to somewhere much bigger than ourselves. It is where we must begin.

SETTING AN INTENTION FOR READING

Reading, for me, has always been a joyful practice of learning, opening, transforming old ideas and adding new ones, while growing a relationship with the author. My wish is that reading this book will offer you the same kind of experience.

I recommend that before you begin reading you set an intention. Setting an intention is a valuable practice for everything we do. It gives us something to anchor to when we are creating new habits and our old ones want to take over. It helps us to complete whatever we undertake. I know from experience that it is easy to pick up books, start them, and never finish.

What is it in this moment that you are wanting to hold space for or transform in your life? This is your intention. It could be mental, physical, or emotional growth or healing. It could be a goal you want to achieve for yourself or a prayer for someone you love. Write your intention and today's date inside the front cover. If this is your second or third reading of this book, your intention may be different this time. Write down this new intention and the date.

If you like, create a sacred space where you will read this book—whether that space is physical or mental—and go there each time you read. This could take the form of sitting in your favorite cozy chair, or maybe lighting a candle or incense and taking a moment to take a few deep breaths.

Establishing an intention helps to make the time you spend reading a sacred practice. We do the same at the beginning of a yoga practice. It aligns us with a force bigger than ourselves. It prepares the mind, the nervous system, the will, and the heart for seeing things in a new way, which is the goal of yoga.

INTRODUCTION

In every moment, we can put one of two messages out into the world: either "I need love" or "I am love." If you pause to notice your thoughts and actions, you can most often trace them back to one of these two seed thoughts.

"I need love" stems from the illusion that we are alone and separate. We search outside ourselves for the next thrill, person, or situation that could heal the void we feel in the heart. Yet this searching only deepens the wound of separateness because it cannot address the underlying conclusion that we are alone. We may feel the effects of this conclusion as hopelessness, stuckness, anxiety, or restlessness.

The times in my life when I have been brought to my knees in hopelessness have all stemmed from loneliness. It was through the practice of yoga that I realized I am not alone, that on the other side of aloneness is all-one-ness. Even during my first attempts to do the awareness practice that I share in this book, training the mind in the power of pause, I realized there is something everlasting that has witnessed every moment of my life. It has tasted every emotion right alongside me, even the emotion of loneliness, yet it has not been affected by it or reacted to it because it has never been lonely.

So also, there is a part of you that has been a witness to your whole life, from birth to this moment. When you learn how to relax into identifying with that part of you and how to align your life choices with it, you discover the part of you that is a continuous, harmonious current echoing "I am love."

It may not seem likely that something as simple and nonmaterial as "I need love" versus "I am love" could affect our well-being and even our health, but it can. The role of love in physical health is beginning to be recognized in Western medicine. The lifestyle medicine program developed by Dean Ornish, MD, for reversing heart disease, for example, is designed to optimize four areas of a person's life. Eating heart-healthy food and exercising are two of these areas. The third is how the person manages stress. The fourth is connectivity—how much love and emotional support the person experiences as both a giver and a receiver.

"I need love" keeps us in a mild state of arousal or agitation, searching for what we believe we don't have. Neurologically, this state engages the sympathetic nervous system, associated with the fight-or-flight response. "I am love" promotes the firing up of the parasympathetic nervous system and what is called the "rest and digest" response, which is crucial for all repair, rebuilding, and healing. Ideally, the body's autonomic nervous system shifts back and forth between the sympathetic and parasympathetic systems according to the context of the moment. But the ongoing stresses of modern-day culture and lifestyle tend to prompt us to become stuck in a low-grade version of fight-or-flight, which can make the mind and body susceptible to illness. Part of the solution, in terms of the nervous system, is to be able to shift into parasympathetic—to find ease, including the deep ease of knowing the truth that at the core, you *are* love. Swami Satchidananda, who began adapting yoga for Westerners and was a teacher of Dr. Dean Ornish, used to say that the difference between illness and wellness lies in the first letters of those two words: "I" and "we."

Some people who have hit the bottom of the "I need love" rabbit hole may begin the search for "I am love," whether they recognize it as that or not. Students show up in my yoga classes, retreats, and trainings because they desire to evolve and become better versions of themselves. They bring with them old habits of self-criticism and undermining their own best interests, of poor self-care or perhaps addictions. However, the desire to be who they are meant to be trumps all in the end. That same desire is what made you open these pages; it is what brings you and me together in this book.

We start on the journey to "I am love" by meeting ourselves where we are in this moment, regardless of our past or our preferences. This moment is the "now" in which yoga always begins. Healing can happen only in the now, the present, not in the past or future. The ancient sage Patanjali, author of the Yoga Sutras, says in Sutra 1.1: "Now is the beginning of yoga" (*atha yoga-anushasanam*).

What is yoga?

The word "yoga" comes from the Sanskrit root *yuj*, which means to yoke, to bring together. Because yoga concerns our individual experience, it is as dynamic as we are. So the word "yoga" has many meanings and interpretations, developed and handed down by different lineages and teachers. Some view yoga as the practice of physical postures (*asanas*). Some say yoga is about the workings of the mind and the movement from lower desires to higher desires. Others say yoga is fundamentally relational. Yoga can mean all of these and more. Like a mirror, yoga will hold different meanings for you along the way as you transform through practice.

I like to say that yoga is the bringing together of all parts of ourselves—physical, energetic, emotional, intellectual—all centered around our essential self, which is Love. When all parts of us align, we radiate the message "I am love." When we are fractionated and not aligned, we are pulled away from our true selves. That estrangement from ourselves is linked with suffering. We fall into the story of "I need love," which is another way of saying I need to find my way home.

The poet T. S. Eliot once defined hell as "a place where nothing connects with nothing."[1] If this is true—and I have experienced this to be true, living through the hell produced by an addictive mind and an eating disorder—then the interconnectedness that yoga brings is a heaven. We create our own hell or our own heaven with our attitudes, behaviors, and choices.

The holistic style of yoga that I teach, Sattva Vinyasa, is rooted in this intention of yoking together all parts of ourselves. It draws upon three ancient Indian traditions: Ayurveda as a source of balance, Tantra as a source of flow, and Yoga as a source of harmony. I think of yoga in terms of harmony because of the alignment it brings to the relationships among the parts of ourselves and our relationships with each other. The musical definition of harmony is two or more notes struck simultaneously, aligning to create a chord with a pleasing effect. In yoga, we are bringing two tones into harmony: living spirit and our human experience. As they align, we move from disharmony or suffering (*duhkha*), to harmony or ease (*sukha*), the goal of yoga therapy.

The yoga tradition offers six main paths to arrive at this state of ease. These are: *karma yoga*, the yoga of selfless service; *bhakti yoga*, the yoga of devotion; *jnana yoga*, the yoga of knowledge and discrimination; *mantra yoga*, the yoga of sound and chanting; *hatha* yoga, the yoga of physical postures; and *raja yoga*, the yoga of reflection and contemplation as outlined in Patanjali's Yoga Sutras. As you understand and learn to embody one path deeply, you will understand and embody all.

This book focuses on yet another yoga path, *kriya yoga*, which Patanjali mentions in the Yoga Sutras. The Sanskrit word *kriya* means "action," and it has other meanings such as purificatory action, practice, movement, function, skill. The focus of Patanjali's Sutras is spiritual liberation, but that means nothing if we don't know how to act in the world. Kriya yoga offers a simple three-step path to awakening while living in the world. Said the other way around, it is a path to engaging in the world with enlightened action. It has worked for me and for my students and clients. And I present my understanding and experience of it here.

Kriya yoga, as Patanjali defines it in Sutra 2.1 of the Yoga Sutras, is made up of three elements, named in Sanskrit *svadhyaya*, *tapas*, and *Isvara pranidhana*. These terms are classically and literally translated as "self-study," "austerity," and "surrender to God." I prefer to interpret them as "awareness," "embodiment," and "surrender" because these words are more accessible to modern-day yoga practitioners, and also because they describe the process of yoga therapy. They form the three foundational steps of the yoga therapy process I teach, as well as the three main parts of this book.

Step 1, awareness, is a process of self-inquiry. It is also the necessary first step toward any kind of healing. We start with becoming aware of our discomfort, our habits (whether physical, mental, or emotional) causing that discomfort, and the values holding those habits in place. In the Indian tradition, the analogy is given of a night watchman who is in the habit of shining his flashlight on what is around him. When we want to see who he is, we must ask him to turn his light on himself. So also, our awareness flows naturally toward the world around us, but we can also direct our awareness toward ourselves. When we do, we become aware of the conditioned responses, the automatic reactions that drive our behavior, as well as the underlying values or conditions that hold those responses in place. Our responses are conditioned by memory, imagination, and wrong knowledge, which have in turn been colored by our fears, attachments, and aversions. By directing our awareness inward, we also get glimpses of our spirit, or higher self, which is beyond and free of this conditioning.

As we become aware of how the conditioning limits us, we naturally want to break free of it. Having observed our habitual patterns long enough to become fed up with the ones that don't serve us, we turn to engage in yogic practices—physical yoga postures (*asana*) and breathwork (*pranayama*) but also working with our thoughts, emotions, and intentions—that help us to break free of those habits by laying down new habits that are more in line with our higher nature. This is Step 2, embodiment.

In the yoga tradition, as said in Yoga Sutra 1.12, the necessary companion of practice (*abhyasa*) is acting without expectations about the results (*vairagya*). Through doing our practices without an agenda, we discover the capacity to let go, which is the marker of Step 3, surrender. Every spiritual path calls upon us to surrender to something greater than ourselves, whether it be God, our higher self, a path, or a trusted teacher. With surrender, the ego gives way a little, which allows us to begin to remember who we really are.

For modern-day Americans, the idea of surrender as a foundational step in yoga therapy and on a healing path may come as a surprise. However, it makes sense because we are complex, multilevel beings, and being estranged from ourselves and our world causes stress, which science has identified as a primary cause of disease (dis-ease). Surrender is one of the states in which our parasympathetic nervous system turns on. We align with a purpose greater than our own. We connect with others and discover true compassion. We shift from "I" to "we." This is when real healing happens.

The three steps are followed by a fourth phase that is not itself a step of kriya yoga but rather is a moment of integration, *samyoga*. It need not be long for it to make an impression. Once we have touched that place, it becomes a reference point. We have caught the flavor of it—just as once you have tasted a certain dish, you know that taste. This pause is not unlike the pause and breath we take during yoga posture practice when completing one yoga posture before moving into the next. Then we begin again with Step 1, awareness, though at a new level of understanding and skill.

As we move through each step our role or identity shifts. In Step 1, awareness, we take on the identity of a *seer*—the one who is becoming aware. We simply observe our thoughts and behavior without reservation or judgment.

In Step 2, embodiment, the seer becomes a *seeker*, the one who is actively engaged in practices that remove conditioned habits. As seekers, we seek balance among the parts of ourselves and harmony, or alignment, with spirit.*

In Step 3, surrender, the seeker lets go of practices and effort, maybe just for a moment, to realize that he

---

*Yoga Sutra 2.17

or she is the *seen*, the one he or she is seeking. That is, he or she becomes intimately aligned with his or her higher self, which is Spirit or God.

The fourth, integrative phase is characterized by a moment of sight, *drishti*, in which seer and seen merge. In this flash of insight, there is no singular small "i." The big "I" merges, even briefly, with the Light, like a candle flame held up to the sun. We relax into the truth of who we are.*

The three steps of kriya yoga move us sequentially toward greater clarity, greater alignment with our higher selves and with others, allowing more of the light of consciousness to shine through our thoughts and actions. We move gradually from disconnection to oneness, from suffering to ease, until we find ourselves comfortably seated in our higher self, even while engaging with the world. The practical and the mystical walk side by side as we both receive knowledge and taste life.

Each time we move through the three steps, we become more aware, our practice deepens, and we become more surrendered. We move through them sequentially, like the smooth turning of the spokes of a revolving wheel. Yet as we progress on the yoga path, we also discover how to move through all three simultaneously. Awareness becomes a form of deeply listening to ourselves, from which flow our right, or *dharmic*, actions in the world, which we do with an attitude of service to others and surrender to Spirit.

*Yoga Sutra 2.21

How each person cycles through the steps will differ. Some of us have more veils (forms of resistance) to work through in a given time period, others may have thinner veils and are already very aware and "in-sightfull." Or it's not yet time for them to work with the thicker veils. I observe this in teacher training courses. Even though everyone takes the same classes and gets the same information, each one comes out of the course differently, according to their readiness to engage in self-study and the practices, and their readiness to receive the material. We each have our own purpose and path. As Ram Dass said, we're all just "walking each other home."[2]

Woven through this book from beginning to end you will find three kinds of information, like three threads. One thread is the yoga lineage: the teachings of the yoga tradition. Another thread is stories of my own transformation through yoga; these are included to illustrate how the yogic concepts and practices work to bring about well-being. The third thread is practices for you, the reader. These are meant as moments for you to pause, reflect on the information and how you relate to it in both head and heart, and begin to apply it to your life and practice.

If you can, read this book three times—once to understand the ideas, once to notice your thoughts and emotions in response to those ideas, and once to relate to the message "I am love." Footnotes referencing Patanjali's Yoga Sutras have been added for those who are wanting to go deeper into the yoga doctrine on how to be happy or are in a teacher training.

In this book I sometimes refer to God, especially when discussing Step 3, surrender. However, this book does not reflect the teachings of any particular religious tradition. Rather, it is meant to be used alongside your own spiritual practices and beliefs, whatever they may be. When the word "God" or "Divine" or "Lord" appears in the text (as in the prayer that follows here), feel free to interpret that word in your own way. If the word brings up tension in your body, simply notice that tension and where it is coming from. Take from the book only what serves you, and sit with any bigger questions it may raise.

As I say to students at the beginning of every yoga class, let's start with an opening intention, in which we offer up together a prayer for ease and light in the world:

Lord, holding steadfast to Our Light, One Light, let us dive into this world's illusion of darkness, igniting a spark of Light in others while being a container for the One Breath that holds the steady, infinite flame of the heart. Amen.

STEP 1
AWARENESS

For most people most of the time, life is a series of habits or unconscious behaviors, and they tend to flow through their days on autopilot. Think about your drive to work or somewhere else you go frequently—the store, school, the yoga center. How often have you arrived at your destination and not remembered the process of getting there? Similarly, at the end of the day, have you ever wondered: "What exactly happened today?" or "How did the day turn out this way again, when I started the day intending it to be different?" This kind of dilemma is where we find ourselves when we allow our habits to run us. They can ruin us rather than reveal us.

The problem here is not that we have habits. In fact, establishing constructive habits, regularity, and routine in our day is the way we achieve constructive change. The problem is that our habits are often unconscious and unintended, simply reactions to daily stressors. In this reactive state of mind, we give away our power to choose. We allow ourselves to be pushed and pulled around by the ups and downs of life rather than taking actions that express genuinely who we are. We then try to soothe the discomfort of this nonalignment by recreating pleasurable experiences from the past or by anticipating and planning for the future, instead of being in the present moment. Eventually, living in this reactive state wreaks havoc on the body and creates disease, or it suffocates us mentally and emotionally.

> *When we choose to pause and sit with ourselves, we place ourselves in the space of awareness.*

If we are fortunate, the pressure of living an inauthentic life eventually squeezes us enough that we begin to acknowledge that something is wrong, that we are not comfortable. Yoga speaks of this discomfort as *duhkha* (suffering).

Once we acknowledge our discomfort, we have three options: ignore it, avoid it by choosing a distracting action or addictive behavior, or move into it so we can trace it to its root and solve it.* The discomfort is like a warning light coming on in your car—something is not working properly, and you need to decide what to do. You can ignore the warning light and continue to drive until the car breaks down. You can pull over, park the car, and walk or hitchhike to your destination, leaving the problem for another day. Or you can locate the nearest repair shop on your cell phone and take steps to get the vehicle fixed.

*Yoga Sutra 1.31

Ignoring discomfort is difficult, once we are conscious of it. We can try to distract ourselves from it by seeking pleasurable experiences, but such distractions are temporary. Not taking the action that will undo the discomfort puts us in a state of disconnect with ourselves. This is a very painful state in which to live.

The first step in addressing our discomfort is to sit with ourselves and look beneath the surface of who we have built ourselves to be—to become aware of our habits. Once we become aware of what we are doing, we can make changes by establishing new routines that become positive habits. This may be unfamiliar territory, so we need guidance and support. Just as once we get our car to the repair shop the next step is to pop the hood and shine a light on the problem with the help of a trained mechanic, so we look for expert support for looking into ourselves—a teacher, a spiritual practice, or a path such as yoga.

When we choose to pause and sit with ourselves, we place ourselves in the space of awareness. The Sanskrit word for the first step of kriya yoga is *svadhyaya*, meaning contemplation, reflection, or study (*adhyaya*) of oneself (*sva*). I call the first step "awareness" as a reminder that the light with which we look at ourselves is the same light of awareness that shines through our higher self.* As we begin to direct that light of awareness at ourselves to see where the suffering is coming

---

*Yoga Sutra 2.1

from and what it is asking of us, we step into the role of the seer, or the witness. This is a part of you that has been watching your whole life unfold without judgment or attachment.

Our awareness practice starts formally by placing our body in a comfortable seated position. The Sanskrit word for any seat or seated position is *asana*. In Yoga Sutra 2.46, Patanjali defines *asana* as *sthira sukham asanam*—a (seated) position characterized by steadiness (*sthira*) and ease (*sukha*). *Asana* is also the word for the physical yoga postures. When describing the yoga postures, it refers to having a suppleness to the body, a firmness in the intellect, and a genuine attitude.

I like to think of asana as being comfortably (*sukha*) seated in the center of ourselves, with mind, body, and spirit aligned (*sthira*). Although in this sense asana is our end goal, we also begin by sitting—to do the awareness practice. However, when we begin this practice, we may find ourselves sitting with ourselves in a certain amount of discomfort. As we observe ourselves over time with the help of this practice, we may realize that we are no longer comfortable with our unskillful ways of behaving with our partners, at work, with ourselves. We may see the loneliness, separateness, or other undesirable emotions that underlie and have been driving those dysfunctional and unconscious habits. This work of viewing our unskillful habits and addictive thought patterns takes courage. The good news is that the discomfort is a sign that we are becoming ready to move beyond this limited way of living.

Most of the time, simply becoming aware of our unskillful habits begins the process of change. This is because our focused awareness, our attention, is our power. The power of attention was made clear to me in 2010, when I led my first yoga retreat to Belize. We took a tour of the cave Actun Tunichil Muknal. I am usually afraid of dark, cold, damp places, but I found it beautiful and enchanting.

We came to a place in the tour six hundred feet down where a plant was growing in complete darkness. How was this possible? The guide told us that the plant's seed had been deposited there in the excrement of a fruit bat. With just a little soil and water from the cave, it was able to sprout. But six hundred feet down in a cave, where was the light it needed to survive? The guide had us turn off our headlamps. It was completely black. We turned them back on, and he said, "It is your light that makes it grow." There were hundreds of tours like ours each month. With all the tour groups stopping to shine their light on this plant, of course it would grow, even thrive.

Think about the things you pay attention to. Many times our attention is drawn to people we disagree with or to circumstances in our lives that we can't change, and we forget to direct our attention to the things we can change. Ask yourself this question, "Does my mind revolve around worry and fear, or do I focus my thoughts on the things I want to grow in my life?

Like the plant in the cave, even if we begin with a pile of shit, there is possibility for growth. Even if you are beginning from a place of chaos and hopelessness, as I did, just choosing to place your attention on yourself in the present moment can be enough for suffering to begin to ease.

The Awareness Practice

Tension is who you think you should be. Relaxation is who you are.
  – Chinese proverb

To cultivate the role of the seer and the capacity for self-observation, it is useful to have an awareness practice and to do it often, so self-reflection becomes a constructive habit. I use the following awareness practice myself and also with clients in yoga therapy sessions.

This awareness practice draws from the yoga tradition's *panchamaya* model, which describes five levels of human experience. The five levels, ranging from more gross to more subtle, are our physical body (*annamaya*);

our energy (*pranamaya*), which includes our breath; our lower mind (*manomaya*), which includes the emotions; our higher mind (*vijnanamaya*), or intellect and intuition; and our freedom or bliss body (*anandamaya*), through which we experience the joy and expansiveness of our true nature.

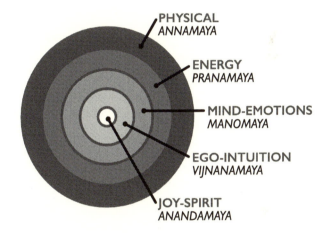

The awareness practice focuses on the first three levels of the panchamaya model only: the physical, energetic, and mental/emotional, since these are the levels most apparent to us, and our experiences are likewise always entwined physically, mentally, and emotionally. For example, if you have a sore back, your energy may be constricted and you may feel irritable, angry, or depressed. So also, if you are depressed, eventually this will affect your energy and your physical body, causing physical pain such as a sore back and perhaps restriction of breath.

Have someone read the following to you out loud as you do the practice, or read each paragraph to yourself and then reflect upon it. Or record yourself reading it and then listen to the recording as you do the practice.

The Awareness Practice

Take a comfortable seat in a position in which you can feel relaxed and also supported. This could be in a chair, on the floor against a wall, or elevated on a bolster with your spine upright, as if you were balancing a book on the crown of your head. Relax your shoulders softly—you may feel a spreading across the collar bones and upper chest.

Notice your breath and any sensation or shape change the breath causes in your body. Which is longer, your inhale or your exhale? If one is more strained or difficult than the other, just notice.

Now, begin to visualize each inhale flowing in through the nostrils, pouring first down to the navel and then steadily filling the chest up through the sternum (breast bone) by the top of the inhale. Notice each exhale relaxing the back of the body as the breath moves all the way up from the navel and out of the nostrils again. At the end of the exhale, allow a slight pause in the breath as the pelvic floor lifts slightly. If exhaling through the nostrils is difficult, exhale through pursed lips. With patience, notice the pauses at the end of the inhale and at the end of the exhale, while maintaining the connection to the earth through your firm and supple seat.

Next start to move your awareness through the physical body, beginning at the feet. (Note: If you have pain in the head or upper body, then begin from the head and move the awareness down to the feet.)

If you sense discomfort somewhere along the way, notice what that discomfort really feels like. Is it changing or consistent? Warm, dull, or sharp? Say an internal "hello" to the sensation and then move your attention on to the next point of awareness. If you sense a place of pleasure, notice what the pleasure really feels like. Is it changing or consistent? Warm, dull, or sharp? Is the body holding both pleasure and pain? Both tension and relaxation?

Slowly move your awareness upward from the feet to the ankles. Then to the shins. The knees. The thighs. The hips. The pelvis. The lower back, then the middle back, then the upper back. The chest. The shoulders. The upper arms. The forearms. Then the wrists and down to the tip of each finger. Then back up the arms to the neck, the jaw, the cheeks, the eyes, and the forehead.

Take in the picture of your physical body as a whole.

Pause and reflect briefly on what you are noticing about the body's sensations.

Now switch your attention to your energy, as if you were changing the channel on a television screen. You are still aware of the physical body—the channel you were previously focusing on—but now you are placing your attention on your energy. Notice how you feel. Elevated and excited? Dull and heavy? Somewhere in between? Perhaps simply calm and relaxed? What is your energy like in this moment?

Pause and reflect briefly on what you are noticing about your energy.

Now shift your awareness to your thoughts, again as if you were changing channels. You are still aware of the physical and energetic levels of your human experience, but you are now viewing the mind. As you shift the light of awareness to your thoughts, does the mind become quiet or more active, or even reactive?

Notice what you are thinking. Begin to sort your thoughts as you would sort the items in your recycling bin. Label each thought—for example, "planning," "judging," "imagining," "worrying," and so on. Once a thought is labeled, let it go, as if you were filing it away. Are any repetitive thought patterns arising?

Pause and reflect briefly on what you are noticing about your thoughts.

Now, as if you were tuning into yet another channel, while remaining aware of the others, turn your awareness to any emotions you might be experiencing. Be courageous and welcome your emotions, whatever they are in this moment. Notice if you are experiencing any physical sensations connected to your emotions. If you are, where are these sensations occurring? How do they feel?

> Pause and reflect briefly on what you are noticing about your emotions.
>
> Now return your awareness to the physical body. Notice the sensations. What has changed? What has stayed the same?
>
> Notice once again where your body touches whatever is supporting you as you are seated. Has your relationship to where you are in this moment changed?
>
> Open your eyes.
>
> As you leave your seat and return to your day, notice if your perspective has changed.

Deepening Our Awareness

Practice is the way to develop skill in any art form. Doing the awareness practice every day creates a ritual for developing our awareness as a crucial tool for progressing on the yoga path. It is a perfect practice to do immediately upon waking—checking in with your body, energy, thoughts, and emotions as you start your day. You can do it while you are still in bed, using the snooze button to dedicate time for this exercise rather than for six more minutes of sleep.

By making the awareness practice a habit, we cultivate, among other things, the power of pause, which is so lacking in our modern, industrialized society. Pausing to look within shifts us out of the reactive state of mind and into a reflective state. Physiologically, it flips the switch from the sympathetic nervous system, which governs the body's fight-or-flight response, to the parasympathetic nervous system, the one that governs the rest-and-digest response. The parasympathetic system releases healing hormones into the blood that improve all the organ functions, including digestion, mood, and behavior. In that restful state, it is also easier to be aware and to be present. It is only when we are in a parasympathetic response that healing can happen.

When we are in a reactive state of mind, we are identifying with what is changing as if it were our entire reality. It is as if we were on a Ferris wheel—when we are up, we are really up, and when we are down, we feel like we are being crushed under the wheel. In a reflective state of mind we are better able to move to the center of the wheel, as it were, from where we can witness the ups and downs of life without identifying with them as our entire experience. At the center there is more ease, and we can begin to see what is. This is the ease (*sukha*) Patanjali talks about in his definition of *asana*. Even in Step 1, awareness, we can get a taste of what it is like to engage in the movement of life while remaining comfortably seated in ourselves.

Just as we use a yoga strap to stretch and tone our bodies, we can use the awareness practice to stretch and tone our attention, so we can place it where we want as long as we want. Becoming aware of all the levels of our human experience, beginning with the physical body, is important for strengthening the mind and accessing higher wisdom. At the end of the awareness practice we return our attention to the body, where we began. Returning to the physical level is a reminder that all parts of us, though in constant flux, are interconnected.

In the awareness practice, there is a moment for observing and sorting through our thoughts, as well as our sensations, energy, and emotions. We can learn to observe our thoughts as if they were clouds moving across a vast, unclouded sky, which is the witness mind, or *buddhi*. We can label them as different kinds of thoughts—planning, judging, imagining, worrying, and so on—which also helps with seeing them objectively.

In the Yoga Sutras (1.5), Patanjali presents an ancient system for sorting thought forms into five kinds. The first kind of thought form is correct knowledge (*pramana*), thoughts that are true to the information taken in by our senses; we are not mistaking what we perceive for something other than it is. The second is incorrect knowledge (*viparyaya*)—for example, concluding that a yoga strap lying on the floor of a poorly lit room must be a snake. The third is imagination (*vikalpa*), which I think of as "the shit I am making up." The fourth and fifth thought forms are deep sleep (*nidra*) and memory (*smriti*).

We don't need to use Patanjali's labeling system. We can use our own labels and still get the benefit from sorting thoughts. Noticing them and setting them aside through labeling is like keeping the surface of a desk clear by sorting and filing away the papers that would otherwise clutter it. Through self-inquiry we can ask questions of our misperceptions and imagination, our dreams and fantasies, such as "Is this really true?" Or "Where did that belief come from?" "Wow, I have been aware only of feeling pain, but there is also a place in my body that feels good."

The awareness practice also provides a space for observing our emotions. Sometimes emotions can be very subtle, and their channel can be hard to pick up. At other times our emotions take over our attention and are the only signal we get, making it hard to see beyond the reactive state they cause.

We must be fierce in our attention and firm with our purpose when working with our emotions. Look your emotions in the eye fearlessly. Emotions are residue from our thought experiences. They can be powerful guides if we drop the stories and memories associated with them and just sit with the experience and sensation of the emotions themselves. This allows us to digest those experiences without replaying the trauma of the past.

> *The more we practice observing our multidimensional nature, the better we are able to notice all levels of our human experience from moment to moment.*

The more we practice observing our multidimensional nature, the better we are able to notice all levels of our human experience from moment to moment. We begin to see how we are taking in, and taking on, the world around us. We become able to notice our habits with some objectivity and to recognize both our skillful and our unskillful behaviors—our habituated patterns and addictions, as well as our unique gifts to be shared with the world. Noticing is a prerequisite to being able to make a conscious change. As we become aware of our habits and patterns, we are able to decide which ones we want to change and which we want to keep.

Awareness of the Seer

One of the gifts of doing the awareness practice is that our awareness deepens and becomes more refined. As we observe how the various levels of ourselves are always in flux, our attention may turn—perhaps in quick glimpses at first—from our behaviors, energy, thoughts, and emotions to the part of us that is doing the observing. This is the seer, the part of us that has been witnessing the flux our whole life. This witness self is associated with the two most subtle layers of the panchamaya model—the higher mind or intellect (*vijnanamaya*) and the expansive freedom body (*anandamaya*) through which the light of the higher self shines.

The more we practice, the better we get at experiencing these subtle levels of ourselves. As we become more aware of them, questions may arise, such as "Who am I?" "Why was I born?" "How can I live fully?" We don't need to look outside ourselves to find the answers to these questions. We have them already. We simply need to remove what is not us to reveal what has always been there.

"Remove" here is not really removing anything. Rather, it involves using a process of discrimination to see through our false identifications. We identify with the physical body: I am short, I am tall, I am tired, I am sunburned. Yet we also perceive the body as other than ourselves, as when we say: I have a body, my body is short or tall, my body is tired. For to call something ours requires seeing it as different from us. We say: I am not my physical body; I *have* a physical body.

According to the yoga teachings, if this discrimination is possible at the physical level, then it is also true at the other levels of the self. For instance: I have a mind, I have thoughts. I am not my thoughts, although the ego would like me to believe I am. Similarly, I can identify with my emotions: I am angry. But I can also say: I am experiencing anger. We have emotions, but we are not our emotions. Emotions are simply subtle forms of thought and energy that move through us, allowing us to experience the variety of colors that are emotions as if they were painted on the canvas of awareness.

We can continue to peel away identification with the various layers that are always in flux until we rest in what is permanent about us, which is consciousness, Light.

Aligning Our Actions with Our Values

True freedom is where an individual's thoughts and actions are in alignment with what is true, correct, and of honor—no matter the personal price.
– Bryant H. McGill

As we develop self-awareness through practice, one important area of ourselves to study is our values. A behavior, especially a habitual one, tends to be supported by a corresponding value. Under an unskillful behavior, there is often a dysfunctional assumption or a fear.

Knowing our values is important because what we think we value and the actions we take can conflict, even if unconsciously, which means we are out of integrity with ourselves. We may be walking around wearing our values like badges of honor on our sleeve without having assimilated them.

For example, perhaps honesty is one of our values, but we avoid speaking up about a problem that needs addressing because of fear of confrontation. We may value being honest with ourselves, but to get through a difficult moment we may turn to cigarettes or alcohol rather than letting the pain of the moment bring us closer to who we are. We might do less than we said we would and then seek out a reward to make us feel better about the task half done, as in doing only half of a run and then telling ourselves it's okay to eat an extra slice of cake.

Aligning our actions with our values is a form of self-reverence. It is often said that you have to love yourself before you love others. When we are clear about what our values are and our daily actions reflect them, we feel heroic for keeping our word to ourselves.

One of the best ways to test the strength of your values is to come up against your unconscious beliefs and behaviors. Let me share an incident in which I learned this, as I was acting out of fear, not love.

One beautiful summer day, I was just diving into some coconut ice cream topped with granola, following a lunch of kale, red radish, and raw goat cheese, when I was interrupted by a knock at the door. I could see through the window an unfamiliar African American, middle-aged man standing on the porch, gazing in at me, stern faced.

I live in a neighborhood where the population ranges from artists and baby boomers to people living on unemployment or selling drugs. I love the diversity and unpredictability. But I was not up for a surprise this afternoon. In fact, I felt cautious and somewhat afraid.

I slowly opened the door, holding my cell phone in one hand, as every possible dire news headline flashed through my mind. I took a deep breath and tried to look the man straight in the eye. "How can I help you?"

> *Aligning our actions with our values is a form of self-reverence.*

The man asked if my husband was home.

"No," I said hesitantly.

He proceeded to tell me that my husband had promised him work and that he would like to mow our lawn. I looked around but did not see a lawnmower. So I said nothing. He then explained that times were hard for him and his wife, whom I could see standing on the sidewalk, stone-faced and wiping the sweat from her brow.

"We have had a hard time putting food on the table," he said, "and the food stamps won't arrive until next week. We are hungry. Please help us out."

Our eyes met again, and for a moment we saw ourselves reflected in one another's gaze. I could see how he viewed me: a privileged white chick. He could see how I viewed him: an ungrateful freeloader.

Bristling inside, I told him to wait a moment while I grabbed something for them from the kitchen. I wanted to help them—I help people, right?—but I also wanted to end our exchange as soon as possible. I came back with some veggies, rice, and a can of organic beans—the healthy organic food would do them some good, right?

By now, the man had rejoined his wife on the sidewalk, so I came outside onto the porch. The man looked at what I had in my hands, waved his arms at me in aggravation, and said, "Seriously, you expect that to fill us up? Look at us! We was hoping for some McDonald's or something!" They turned and walked away, waving at me in disgust.

I was left standing on my front porch holding my thirty-dollar organic, skinny-bitch yoga food, my inner being in turmoil. I was angry about the intrusion in the first place, and then about the insult of their throwing their arms up at me. How could this ridiculous person possibly appreciate the person he had turned down, someone with ten years of yoga and Ayurveda study? I was also sad. This person and I could not meet because the layers of our personalities were so thick—mine steeped in self-righteous giving and his in "you owe me something better."

Gradually, as I processed this experience through the afternoon and evening, my perspective shifted. I saw that I had been unable to find kinship with this person because of my assumptions about who he was, my assumptions about myself, and my conditioned fears. Because of this conditioning, I had not been able to see the way he needed to receive love. We can do violence when we love people the way we think they should be loved rather than meeting them where they are and loving them the way they understand love.

If I had been in line with love as one of my values, instead of letting fear have its way, I might have taken a different path of action. Maybe I could have handled the situation differently. So what if they wanted McDonald's? I could have given them enough money for a couple of Big Macs. I could have walked down the street with them, bought them a meal, and gotten to listen to their story.

The experience left me humbled. To some observers, it may have looked like I was right and he was wrong. But yoga is a moment-to-moment practice. In that moment, I got to see how my actions had stemmed from haste, fear, and judgment.

As we start to view our behaviors in light of our values, we see that we have the power to choose how we respond to the world. At any moment, we may stand at a crossroads of what to align with: embodying love or reacting to fear. We can choose to let our values shape our intentions. As I like to say to students and clients, intention without action is fantasy and action without intention is fallacy.

Yoga's Universal Values

Consciousness begins with an act of defiance.
– Carl Jung

Often, the values we think are our own have been handed to us by the people and the culture around us—parents, teachers, friends, our workplace, even the media. Some of the "shoulds" we carry may be the values of teachers or family members whose views we accepted without questioning. However, we have the opportunity to decide which values are truly valuable to us. This may mean bulldozing some of the values of the tribe we were raised with and replacing them with other values. This process begins with awareness, and it can take some careful thought.

What values do we want to choose? The yoga system, like all spiritual paths, offers us universal values to live by. They are universal because they are aligned with the greater good. They are founded on love and truthfulness, which are inclusive. All people respond to these universal values, even if they live their lives denying them. If a criminal walked into a restaurant and took a seat next to the Dalai Lama, something would shift inside the criminal just by being in the presence of someone who has assimilated values such as virtue, faith, and righteousness to such a high degree.

Choosing to live by a universal value connects us with all beings. If we choose to live by a value that serves only ourselves, it is like watering just one spot in the lawn; the rest of the lawn will eventually die. When we focus on a universal value, it is like watering every blade of grass, including our own.

Yoga packages universal values as precepts, or guidelines, for living. The *yamas* and *niyamas* outlined in Patanjali's Yoga Sutras are among the best known, but there are others. I discuss some of them in Step 2. Just as the physical practice of yoga brings our bones and muscles into alignment, so practicing the precepts of yoga brings our personal values into alignment with universal values.

The process of examining our behaviors, breaking down our old habits, and building new ones that are aligned with our values happens over time. It's a messy process, and it can get messier before we arrive where we want to be. There can be turmoil in the mind as we notice the disconnect between action and value: wow, that was not my intention. It's like cleaning and organizing a closet—it becomes even more of a mess as you pull everything out of the closet to sort through it. However, eventually the clutter is gone and the closet is in order.

With our values clarified, we can then make more authentic choices about how we act in the world, rather than react. Then our life purpose—which in Sanskrit is called our *dharma*—will unfold like the blossoming of a flower.

> ### Becoming Aware of Our Values
>
> Take a moment to contemplate where there may be misalignment between your values and your actions.
>
> Make two lists on a piece of paper or your computer. On one, write down the values you hold. As you write, you may realize that some or all of them were instilled in you by peers, family, or religion. On the other, write down the actions you do as a daily routine.
>
> Compare the two lists. Notice if how you are spending your day is aligned with your values. Notice which actions support your values and which actions do not.
>
> Think of each value as the bull's-eye and your actions as arrows. If one of my values is to eat healthfully but I order carryout several times a week, I will not hit the bull's-eye. If my value is community but I often avoid groups, what action would I be comfortable taking to target that bull's-eye?
>
> Is one of your values not represented on the list of actions? What actions could you take regularly to express that value? Add that to the list.
>
> Do some of the actions on the list fail to reflect any of your values? How could you modify those actions so they are in line with your values? If they do not reflect your values, draw a line through them.

Look now at the list of actions (except the ones crossed out) and begin to visualize these as new routines in your day that support your values.

STEP 2
EMBODIMENT

We may take up the practice of yoga to achieve a desired result, such as to heal our body, to relieve stress, to quiet the monkey mind, or just for the pleasure of it, but yoga can give us far more. Its greatest gift is insight into ourselves. Through doing the awareness practice, we can reach a quiet, reflective state in which we become aware of our unconscious, conditioned thoughts and behaviors. We begin to see that those thoughts and behaviors are part of a reactive state of being, in which our actions tend to be driven by ego, likes and dislikes, and the desire to appear a certain way or achieve a certain outcome. This reactive state of being occurs when the sympathetic nervous system is firing. It is not favorable for healing or for habit change.

In that state of calm reflection, we can also glimpse what it's like to live free from conditioned thoughts and behaviors. We realize that we can actually choose to be in a responsible (response-able) state of being. I like to say that to respond instead of react is to Act with a capital A—that is, to act with higher intention, in alignment with the higher mind, or *buddhi*, and with the universal values. From this nonreactive state of being, we are able to choose the right action for the moment and to engage in more skillful, rather than preprogrammed, behaviors. This experience gives us a sense of new freedom and ease in our being as well as in our bodies.

The question I often hear from my students as they reach this point of greater awareness is "What can I do to maintain that freedom?" The answer is always this: practice. This kind of freedom is not something we achieve once and it's done. To make living responsibly a habit requires daily practice, which is the focus of Step 2.

As we begin to see that the practice of yoga can actually help to free us from our conditioned behavior, we feel drawn to deepen our practice. As we commit more fully to our practice we also shift out of the role of *seer* to become a *seeker*. The seer is the part of us that becomes aware of our habitual conditioning and our freedom. The seeker puts that awareness into action. Another way of describing this shift is that we move from being yoga practitioners to becoming yogis.

The Sanskrit word for Step 2 of kriya yoga is *tapas*, which literally means heat. To practice is to move against the grain of our habits. This creates friction, or heat.

Tapas also means discipline or austerity. The "heat" of tapas burns off a layer or two of the false self that we have been presenting to the world due to fear or loneliness and moves us more into alignment with our true self.

Tapas begins at the point where doing the comfortable thing you have always done becomes no longer tolerable and doing what is uncomfortable becomes the means for transformation. The seeker is ready and willing to come up against his or her own unskillful thoughts and actions, the way a yogi standing tall in mountain pose at the beginning of asana practice is willing and ready to move into the other asanas.

While the common translation of *tapas* is discipline, my favorite way of interpreting tapas is embodiment. I often imagine the principle of tapas as a form of spiritual gravity. Just as the gravity studied in physics is the fundamental force that connects us to the planet, so spiritual gravity is a force that grounds us in the body.

When our actions are grounded in the body, we begin to move with what science is recognizing as our enteric brain, referring to the complex of five hundred million neurons in our gut. By connecting to this brain in our gut, we can learn the language of this "inner knowing" of trusting our gut, our body response, and let this intrinsic wisdom guide us on our path.* As David Hawkins explains in his book *Power vs. Force*, we can

---

*Yoga Sutra 2.43

access a simple yes/no answer to any question we have through our body response.

Part of the work of yoga therapy is helping people get back in touch with their physical bodies through yoga therapies, such as asana, pranayama, and meditation. The physical body can be a means for releasing old stories and trauma stored in the lower mind, which may be the source of conditioned responses. When we are grounded in the body, we are also grounded in the present moment and for creating new memory impressions. Attuning ourselves to the gravity of the present moment allows us to be more aware of our actions. Then we are able to embody universal values by choosing to engage in more skillful behaviors. Our movements in the world then change also, and we become a vessel for service in the world (*karma yoga*). Hence this pillar of kriya yoga is the pillar of transformation.*

> *Yoga is about going against the grain in a relaxed way.*

To go against the grain of our habits takes energy. It also takes courage. It requires us to say yes when our mind wants to take the easy no, and to say no when our mind wants to take the easy yes. I always tell people that the hardest part of asana practice is making it to the mat or the yoga studio. But once we are there, and once we decide to move through the poses, even the poses we dislike, we find deeper and deeper acceptance and peace.

*Yoga Sutra 4.34

At the same time, going against the grain does not mean fighting with ourselves. Often when making changes, we try to make them with an approach of "no pain, no gain," which is the stress response and why our change doesn't stick. Yoga is about going against the grain in a relaxed way. To go against the grain of an unskilled habit, we must tap into something greater than our small self, the part of the mind that identifies with worldly appearances and ego. Through doing the awareness practice, we get a glimpse of our higher self, and because it is our real nature, we begin to relax into it and to act from there.

When we are acting from this relaxed, aware place, which is the core of our being, we are acting in the present moment. The Sanskrit word *atha*, meaning "now," is the first word of Yoga Sutra 1.1: "Now the instruction of yoga begins" (*atha yoga-anushasanam*). When we are in the present moment, we are practicing yoga. The more we remain centered in the present, the more we begin to embody the practices of yoga both on and off the mat. Then the world becomes a sacred space for our yoga practice, a living school of yoga.

How to Practice: Making Action Sacred

The most selfless person is the most selfish person, because by being selfless you keep yourself happy and peaceful always.
— Swami Satchidananda

In Yoga Sutra 1.12, Patanjali introduces two principles on which the entire system of yoga rests. One is *abhyasa*, meaning practice and persistent effort. The other is *vairagya*, which is often translated as nonattachment.

In our culture, nonattachment is often understood as pushing something away. But vairagya is not about rejecting or abstaining. It is about arriving in the present moment without an agenda. Rather than a disengaging, it is a fullness of embracing and reconciliation. When considered together with its word pair, abhyasa, I like to think of vairagya as holding our practice in an agendaless space. When we act without an agenda, we begin to see that the outcomes of our actions are not in our control. What happens is in the hands of a greater will than our own. When viewed this way, our actions become sacred.

Whether we act with or without an agenda concerns not so much the actions we undertake but more the intention behind the actions. It is our intention, not our actions, that creates our *karma*, which is the mental and spiritual residue of our actions.*

*Yoga Sutra 2.14

Karma can be positive or negative, depending on whether our actions are aligned or not aligned with universal values. The quality of our karma creates our feelings about ourselves and others and lays the foundation for our future—whether it will be happy or not. One way to keep our karma clear and our hands clean is to remove our personal agenda from our actions.

Our agendas most commonly show up in relationship to others. People can sense when someone has an agenda. We can't feel other people's physical pain, but we can feel when they have an ulterior motive, just as we can feel when they are angry, sad, or joyful. As the brilliant Maya Angelou said, "People will forget what you said, people will forget what you did, but people will never forget how you made them feel."[3]

A remedy for undoing our agendas about others is to remember that every human life is precious. Don't try to change others; instead, offer your practice up to them. We change others the most by embodying change ourselves.

Have No Agenda about Comfort

The best time to practice any new behavior is when you notice that you are doing the opposite. So also, the best time to practice not having an agenda is when one shows up—when you feel yourself backed into the corner of desire regarding a certain outcome, and you realize that you do, in fact, have an agenda.

For instance, at times I desire comfort. I crave people and things that bring me comfort, or even my fantasies about people or things making me comfortable. I desire a warm bed and more time inside as the weather chills. I long for the warmth of a cup of tea in my hands or a warm body to ground me in solace. Sometimes these things nourish us. We need to ask ourselves if we are trying to avoid change or seeking nourishment.

> *Life doesn't have to be suffering, but at some point it will be, and this is when you become alive.*

Why do we crave comfort? Because we are scared. We fear discomfort, and we fear the unknown—whereas in actuality, the path to truth, to change, to healing, lies in the unknown.

If you are really listening to your inner wisdom, you will find that the journey to the core of your being is mostly uncomfortable, which is why at some point all religions and philosophies speak of life as suffering. Life doesn't have to be suffering, but at some point it will be, and this is when you become alive. In the children's novel *The Velveteen Rabbit*, a stuffed rabbit is made real by a magic fairy—but only after the rabbit understands suffering.

Yoga invites us to become comfortably seated in ourselves, and the way to achieve this is not by avoiding the uncomfortable moments. Beware of spending too much time in your comfort zone, the practices and life circumstances that feel easiest, because usually it means you are allowing the mind to be pulled here and there by the senses. Allow yourself to be rubbed a little by life. The squeeze of life loving you is what creates the momentary pause necessary to be able to see and become who you are.

In the Zen tradition, masters sometimes strike their students with a stick when they least expect it, to induce a moment of alert pause right before the inevitable questions arise: "What the hell just happened? Why did you do that?" While it may be hard for us to wrap our minds around this one (which is precisely the point), if you take a look at your life, isn't it the "WTF" moments that have steered you toward the path of transformation? In the shock of those brief pauses happening outside our comfort zone, we momentarily experience ourselves as pure and free of karma.

> *Allow yourself to be rubbed a little by life.*

The yogis of the past were feared because they were rebels and welcomed the discomfort that the rest of us resist. They knew that every circumstance, especially the ones that are uncomfortable, is for our growth. Welcome the uncomfortable moments that shift you out of your habitual state of mind. If life is comfortable, then it is habitual, and nothing will be shown to you about who you are.

At first, we become seekers because we are suffering and have realized that we can no longer blame our suffering on our brothers and sisters or the world around us. As we continue to seek we loosen our grip on the agenda that we shouldn't have to suffer. Then the only seeking we need to do is to find out how we can serve the person or situation in front of us without needing a reward. Only then can we become compassionate beings.

Instead of thinking of people, things, and warm cups of tea that might comfort us, let us consider the people and things that we bring comfort to: the warm bed that we give purpose to when we place our body on it; the cup of tea that feels our fingers interlaced around it, containing its warmth; the warm body that finds grounding and solace from our embrace.

Practice Nonattachment to the Results

The work we do offers us a perfect opportunity to practice not having an agenda, for work is often structured around achieving results. I am not saying to let go of doing your job well; rather, when you begin each task or process or interaction, let go of your expectations for a certain ideal outcome. When we let go of expectations about the results, we are aligned with the bigger will at hand. So we can become vessels for healing the earth, society, and one another.

Krishna tells Arjuna in the Bhagavad Gita (3.30): "Perform all things for my sake alone, desireless, absorbed in the Self." This is the yoga of action—acting for the sake of someone or something bigger than yourself, which is what makes our actions sacred. If not for God's sake, then do your work for the sake of those you love. Start there. Most of us find it easy to love animals, children, nature. Offer your work to them, and it will become a spiritual practice (*sadhana*).

Most religions advise us in some way not to "eat the fruit," whether literally or figuratively in the sense of the fruits of our actions. We plant a seed, wait for the fruit to show, and watch it ripen. Then we might think, "It is perfect. Maybe I can have just a taste to see what I have created." But if we leave the fruit alone, it will fall from the tree, scattering seeds upon the earth from which new trees will sprout, multiplying the good in our original action.

It is always easier to seek instant gratification and take credit, or "eat the fruit," so we can say we had a good day. But collecting rewards for doing good works is a gilded cage that confines us nonetheless. When we act in a way that is not lined up with our true self, the effect of that action stays with us.

Not having an agenda is one of the things I speak about the most when training yoga teachers and yoga therapists. Yoga teachers often receive emails thanking them for helping people find a new direction. Let me tell you a secret: we're not the ones creating change. Yoga works. We don't even have to call it yoga. Simply being true, kind, and present with one another can promote healing where it is needed.

In my work as a yoga therapist, there is inevitable satisfaction when a back is strengthened, pain is managed, or quality of life is improved, especially when the client is also going through treatment for cancer or addiction. However, at the end of the day, I get to practice leaving all that behind.

I received an email some time ago telling me how much I had changed a student's life. Yes, I love these emails. My ego really wanted to hang on to it, stash it away for a "rainy day"—a time when I would be feeling bad about myself or feeling lonely—or maybe as a "get out of jail free" card to justify straying from the path a bit. However, I knew in that moment of gratitude that the reward was not mine to keep. I replied with a thanks-filled email and congratulated the student on making the change in her life she had intended to make. Then I had to let it go so our relationship as student and teacher, and my relationship with my life purpose, would remain clean.

One of my first yoga teachers said that karma means you can't get away with shit. In other words, when our actions are out of line with our values, their effects stick to us. So also, if we decide it is okay to lie or do harm, just this once—sometimes just because it makes us feel alive—it really does leave an imprint on the world. And it creates a big, deep pile of personal shit.

But when we act as a vessel and feel ourselves to be part of the whole, no trace of karma clings to us, for there is no reward for us to cling to. We are simply resting comfortably in our true nature, in our sacred seat.

A good way to become less attached to the results of our actions is to cultivate a meditation practice. Meditation cleanses the mind of our likes and dislikes, of our preferences for sweet over bitter, for success over failure. It helps us resolve the opposites.

The *Mundaka Upanishad* describes two birds dwelling in the same tree. One jumps from branch to branch tasting the various fruits, both bitter and sweet. The other sits quietly observing the other bird. The observing bird is the witness self, and the experiencing bird is the mind. The witness self is the one we make contact with and then awaken when we cultivate a meditation practice.

Trying to bring the mind to a state of focused meditation is a lot like trying to fall asleep. The more we try to make it happen, the more elusive it becomes. This is why a meditation practice is mostly preparing the mind for the state of meditation. For this reason, I like the idea of calling it a sitting practice.

Cultivating a Sitting Practice

Plan your sitting practice the way you would plan a trip. Research the technique that resonates with you, choose your object of focus, make a plan that is realistic, and know that you may encounter some turbulence on the way.

Travel advisory: Getting to the cushion is always the hardest part.

Support your practice by doing it in a space that is comfortable and uplifting. You do not have to sit crossed-legged on the floor, but you do need to try to get your spine elevated and supported. If you are reclining, you may drift into relaxation and sleep, which are good in their own right, but are not meditation. If the spine is not supported by a chair or by the strength of your back from practicing asana, it will be more difficult to concentrate and to breathe fully, or you may experience more physical discomfort. So take some time to establish a comfortable seat.

Schedule your sitting practice at a time that easily fits into your daily schedule. Morning is best for most people. If your habit is to hit the snooze button on the alarm, decide to spend those ten minutes in meditation instead. In the morning the mind is usually fresh and uncluttered from the residue of the thoughts and interactions of the day. Another advantage of morning meditation is that it establishes a good foundation for the entire day. However, whatever time of day you choose is perfect if you can make it a regular practice.

> Once you arrive on your cushion, act as if you were on vacation. Prepare yourself for an adventure into the mind. You may notice a lot of mental static, perhaps only because you have become quiet enough to listen. Appreciate the beauty of the interior landscape. Simply sit with whatever chaos or activity or stillness is in your mind, continually letting go of any judgments that arise. When we are at the beach, we do not ask the sea to be bold or calm; we just appreciate the vast beauty that it is. So also, do not ask your mind to be one way or another; just watch the waves of the mind.
>
> On this trip you will likely encounter detours along the way—physical pain, emotions, to-do lists that call for your attention. Notice the call but then keep bringing your attention back to now. The noticing is a practice of awareness, and bringing your focus back is a practice of mindfulness. Every time you bring yourself back to now through awareness and mindfulness, you are strengthening the salience network of the brain. The salience network, which is located in the insular cortex, plays a role in numerous cognitive functions related to perception, emotion, and interpersonal experience.

By waking early to sit and simply observe the thought fluctuations of the mind, we are devoting a few moments of our time to align with ourselves, with others, and with our Higher Power. When we do this regularly, our whole life can begin to change. Maybe it is because we notice that we need to get to bed a little earlier. Or we may choose to give up wine or heavy foods before bed, so we can wake up lighter to meditate. Or maybe we greet our partner or family in the morning, after our sitting practice, with clearer eyes.

A sitting practice also changes our unconscious patterns by developing new layers of awareness and rewiring our nervous system. Herbert Benson and his colleagues did some of the first research on meditation, which they termed the "relaxation response." They discovered a host of benefits we receive from it. According to their findings, which they report in *The Relaxation Response*, meditation

- lowers oxygen consumption;
- decreases respiratory rate;
- increases blood flow and slows heart rate;
- increases exercise tolerance in heart patients;
- leads to a deeper level of relaxation;
- helps to lower high blood pressure;
- reduces anxiety attacks by lowering levels of blood lactate;
- decreases muscle tension (and any pain due to tension) and headaches;
- builds self-confidence;
- increases serotonin production, which influences mood and behavior;

- helps in chronic diseases like allergies and arthritis;
- reduces premenstrual syndrome;
- helps in postoperative healing;
- enhances the immune system by increasing the activity of natural killer (NK) cells, which kill bacteria and cancer cells;
- reduces the activity of viruses; and
- increases physical and mental strength, calmness, and peacefulness.

Set an Intention

Our agenda is usually created by our ego and is attached to our personal story, or a *vikalpa*—something we make up ourselves and then think is real. The opposite of vikalpa is *sankalpa*, intention. One way to let go of our personal agenda is by engaging a universal value as our intention. Universal values such as generosity, peace, love, truth, and kindness resonate with us because they are the core of who we are.

> *Setting an intention for something you are going to do is like identifying the center of a flower from which all the petals extend outward.*

Setting an intention for something you are going to do is like identifying the center of a flower from which all the petals extend outward. All parts of that action are connected to that intention. And the intention holds your attention steady within the sacred space of a chosen universal value.

Even though it takes time to develop the skill of setting an intention and maintaining it throughout an activity, intention setting is something we want to incorporate early in our yoga practice. The thread of intention should run deep.

Patanjali says in Yoga Sutra 1.14 that yoga practice should be done over a long period of time, uninterrupted, and with full enthusiasm. When setting intentions, we should work with a single intention uninterruptedly for a long time and with full enthusiasm, until we finally embody it. There is a saying: if you dig many shallow wells, you may never find water. The same is true if we work with one intention for only a short time. It is easy in our world of social media and fads that come and go, or even attending yoga classes of varying lineages, for our attention to be drawn in multiple directions. Go deep with one intention until you see it take hold. Work with it until you see it weaving through all aspects of your life.

The first intention I worked with was *truth*—not breaking the promises I made to myself. Truth can be a bit fierce to work with, as it tends to tear down beliefs, addictions, attitudes, and environments that are no longer serving us or perhaps never did. I spent seven years placing the intention of truth in the center of my practices before I felt like I was becoming aligned with truth.

The next intention I set was to be a vessel, to align with something bigger than me. I felt as if truth were the bulldozer that had cleared out the wreckage, and now I could serve others from a clean container. So I prayed for that container to be filled with knowledge and compassion greater than my own, so I could serve without needing the reward of knowing I was helping. It was during this phase that I became a teacher and yoga therapist.

Through the intention of becoming a vessel, which I practiced for three years, my life became very full—so full, in fact, that it grew chaotic. Creativity flowed, and with it came abundance but also busyness and stress. I was having a hard time holding all of the creative energy. Yet from this chaotic epicenter flowed an authentic expression of my dharma, from where I was ready to show up and teach. So gratitude became the next intention I focused on. My practice became this: each time I felt myself getting caught up in the chaos, I would ground my feet on the earth and imagine myself full of gratitude.

One day I was running down the stairs in a panic to get everything done, when I felt a pull beneath me—the way a receding wave pulls the sand underneath your feet when you are standing on the shore—and a wave of blissful gratitude washed over me. I had been doing the gratitude practice often enough that the physiological cues of being grateful were becoming a spontaneous response to stress and overwhelm. This is how it's possible to reprogram our negative reactions and turn them into positive ones.

From the fullness of gratitude I was able to practice generosity. I felt like I was offering something back to the world and contributing to others' lives in an abundant way through the intention of generosity.

I decided to think of this intention as generosity rather than compassion, as I had heard my teacher Robert Thurman describe compassion as simply being generous. At the time, the word "generosity" resonated with me more than the word "compassion," because I was still struggling with my tendency toward people pleasing and, from that place, compassion sounded exhausting, like giving until I was depleted. Generosity felt like a creative energy coming from abundance. From that experience, I realized the importance of choosing the best word for an intention and how personal that choice can be.

My series of intentions were not a set program I had taken from any system. They had come to me simply from listening, as if I were a musician listening for the next note to follow the one that came before. In intention setting we are cocreators with our higher nature, and to be in harmony with our higher nature requires skillful listening on our part. Alignment with this authentic self is inherent in us. If we have not been aligned with it, perhaps we haven't been quiet enough to listen, or we are afraid of failure, or we have been drawn outward into comparison with others.

Failure Is Not an Option

As we begin to put our intention into practice, we will most likely run into obstacles that challenge us, discourage us. Many times, whether we persist in our practice or give up in the face of challenges has to do with our relationship to failure and success. In my teacher-training programs, I ask students to reflect upon what they would do if failure wasn't an option. Some have an immediate response: "Quit my job and travel." "Write a book." "Jump out of an airplane." I call such a response a "big-D desire," something that has been weighing on our heart a long time while something else holds us back from accomplishing that goal. Whatever is holding us back in one area of our life is holding us back in all areas of our life.

Some people are afraid to answer the question because speaking something into being is a powerful practice, and once it is said, the process has begun. It's a big responsibility to speak out loud the life experience we know deep down we are here to have, because it means chopping off the heads of our attachments and fears. And so, the work itself begins.

To answer the question of what you would do if failure was not an option, you must first define what failure means to you. Usually, we are afraid of failure because we are used to a linear, results-driven model of action. Maybe the travel isn't being planned because the person is afraid of not having enough money, or the book isn't being written because the person is afraid of putting himself or herself out there. Maybe fear of death is what's stopping the person from jumping out of a plane. Beware—be aware—of how many unconscious choices stem from the seed of fear.

Fear is necessary to our survival. It can save our lives by prompting us to move out of the path of a fast-moving vehicle. But most of our fears are based in perceived, not actual, danger or in memories of unpleasant moments in the past. Ask yourself: What am I really afraid of? What is the worst that could happen if I fail?

As children, we are not so worried about failure because we tend to see the world as our playground. Most of us are born trusting, and we continue to trust as our basic needs are met. But once someone hurts us or we experience the pain of failure, we become more cautious. We may even stop trying altogether.

As long as our intention remains the foundation of our actions, we cannot truly fail. Look back at the times when you thought you had failed. From the perspective of today, it is often possible to see how those "failures" were actually teachings that led you further down the path to becoming who you are today. If we learn from our perceived failures, then they are really just lessons. If this is true, then we can conclude that failure doesn't really exist. Isn't that a great relief?

Now let me suggest this: if failure doesn't exist, then perhaps success doesn't either.

Sit with that statement for a moment and reflect. How does it make you feel?

Seeking some level of success is typically our motivation for everything we do, our reason to take action. But if there's no failure and no success, then there's nothing to do but act without an agenda, offering up all of our actions.

What to Practice: Skillful Actions

Whether you go up the ladder or down it, your position is shaky.
 – Tao Te Ching, tr. Stephen Mitchell

The second foundational principle of yoga, paired with vairagya (acting without an agenda concerning the results), is abhyasa, regular and constant practice. What do we practice? Skillful behaviors that are aligned with universal values. The nature of practice is tapas—choosing to engage in a certain amount of discomfort in order to achieve the greater comfort, or ease, as that skillful behavior becomes embodied in you. When developing these practices, we may wobble and fall, just as we do when trying to learn a balancing yoga posture. We will no doubt come up against resistance or attachment. But through our commitment to becoming fully who we are, over time we move ourselves into alignment, much as a skilled chess player moves a chess piece into position on a chessboard.

I present here the skillful behaviors I rely on the most as practices for myself and for my students and yoga therapy patients. Each of these practices engages the universal values.

In the eightfold path of yoga as laid out in Patanjali's Yoga Sutras, the practice of ethical precepts comes first, even before the practice of asanas.* For if we are making a mess of our lives, it is much more difficult to move with ease and authenticity in asana practice or to sit comfortably with ourselves in the breath and concentration practices that follow asana. These ethical precepts or practices, the yamas and niyamas, make up the first two steps on the eightfold path. They are the universal principles as taught in the Yoga Sutras. Asana is the third step.

---

*Yoga Sutra 2.29

The yamas and niyamas guide us in developing reverence for ourselves and compassion for others. In the Christian tradition, these practices are summarized in Jesus's teaching to love one another as we love ourselves and to love God above all things.

The yamas are principles and practices concerning the relationship between ourselves and everything and everyone around us. They apply to our actions in the world and throughout our day and life. These practices are truth (*satya*), nonviolence (*ahimsa*), and the values that become assimilated through those two practices: not comparing (*asteya*), moderation (*brahmacharya*), and not grasping or clinging (*aparigraha*).

Once we begin practicing any one of the skillful behaviors, the others naturally follow. However, the first two yamas, truth and nonviolence, are foundational. They can be incorporated into every action we take, where they show up as honesty and love. They are also the answers to two questions we ask ourselves when we realize we are suffering: "Who am I?" and "What should I do?" Love is who we are, and truth is how we should live.

Truth and nonviolence are the two "outer" yamas. As we become more attuned to them and able to embody them, the three "inner" yamas—not comparing, moderation, and not grasping or clinging—show up in our behavior naturally, like the ripening of a fruit.

The niyamas are principles and practices concerning our relationship to ourselves, especially our higher nature in terms of respect, love, and devotion. I like to think of the niyamas as practices for developing self-reverence (which I see as deeper than self-love). Three of the niyamas are the same as the three steps of kriya yoga that form the main topic of this book: awareness (self-study, or *svadhyaya*), embodiment (*tapas*), and surrender to a higher power or our higher nature (*Isvara pranidhana*). For this reason, I won't discuss these three practices as niyamas here.

The other two niyamas are cleanliness (*saucha*) and contentment (*santosha*). Cleanliness as a niyama refers to cleanliness of both body and mind. This is cultivated primarily through asana practice, which prepares us for more advanced practices by balancing our nervous system, which may be overstimulated or understimulated. We use the body and the breath to balance the mind, head, and heart, and through this become more open, sensitive, and aware. It is like cleaning the windshield of your car so you can see where you are heading.

Contentment is not so much a practice in its own right as it is a result of practice. It is the peace we are filled with after doing a balanced yoga practice or when we are living a balanced life. When we are aligned and whole, we are content. Our actions flow from us in love rather than reach out from us in loneliness, as we will explore further in Step 3.

I also include here two practices common to all religious traditions: the practice of treating others with respect, which I call seeing the light in others, and the practice of forgiveness. Respect for others and forgiveness are universal values that become our natural expression as we align

> *Contentment is not so much a practice in its own right as it is a result of practice.*

with our higher nature. As part of our practice in Step 2, they can also be skillful behaviors that we develop and learn.

Finally, I have included four practices that I think of as medicines for the mind. These practices are helpful in addressing fear, egotism, attachment, and aversion, which Patanjali describes as the four branches of the root ignorance that keeps us bound and causes suffering.

The awareness practice must be practiced alongside these skillful behaviors so we develop the witness mind, otherwise known as the buddhi, or higher mind, the part of us that observes what we are doing. For example, it was the witness in me that let me see the nonalignment between my values and my reaction to the man at my door asking for a handout, recognizing the hypocrisy in my actions.

All of these skillful behaviors can be practiced in small, mindful ways as you move through your day. In fact, this is the best way. The time to practice them is not on a yoga retreat or at an ashram, although in those settings we can get a good start. When we temporarily exit our regular life and spend time in a peaceful place, we have time to study and self-reflect. However, the peace we experience there is only simulated. We may strengthen the first step of awareness on retreat, but the time to practice skillful behaviors is once we return home. This is when we are most likely to come up against our reactive, unskillful behaviors—which is the perfect opportunity to choose between our habitual, reactive response and a new behavior, to go against the grain of what is ingrained.

As we practice these skillful behaviors over time, they become assimilated values, not just a system of behaviors we try to follow. Then we are able to be more aware and skillful when a challenge big enough to pull us out of alignment with ourselves comes our way.

> *Truth is a moment-to-moment practice.*

As we begin to make these skillful behaviors our own, we may be tempted to stop practicing them, thinking we have embodied them sufficiently. But no. When we put a skill aside, it fades—just as a musician's performance skills begin to fade if she puts aside her instrument. We must keep these skills sharp through practice, or they become dull weapons that cannot cut through the vines that choke our perception and obscure reality.

The Outer Yamas

Truth without love is brutality, and love without truth is hypocrisy.
— Warren W. Wiersbe

Truth

To live in accordance with truth means to be in integrity with oneself. Have you ever bought a new gym membership, only for it to collect dust as the eighty-dollar-a-month debit continues to draw from your bank account? This is a classic example of the knower-doer split. It is the knower part of you who set the intention and then watched as the doer didn't make it to the gym. When we begin to line up our actions with our values, the seer and the doer become aligned, the way an arrow poised on the bowstring becomes aligned with the bull's-eye of the target.

Every person's truth is their own, dependent on his or her past experiences, perceptions, expectations, and values, both assimilated and handed down. For this reason, I cannot define truth for you. Instead, each of us must define our own truth. This is a process of discovery and discernment.

Truth is a moment-to-moment practice. In every situation we are presented with the question: "What is my truth here and now?" or "What is real here, and what is my most genuine response to it?" Then we can take the action most authentic to us.

Afterwards, take a moment to reflect and assess: "Was that action aligned with my truth?" If it was not, you can use the awareness practice in Step 1 as you sit with the residue of your action. If you find the action was not in line with your truth, do not feel shame or guilt. Simply catch, assess, and release. If you feel resistance, that is actually a good thing. We will feel resistance as we rub up against outdated beliefs and behaviors that are not a reflection of our most genuine self.

By making a regular practice of asking "What is my truth in this moment?" and reflecting on the result, we develop discernment. Eventually, our discernment awakens enough that we can know with certainty what is true for us in each moment. Taking action in alignment with that truth is acting in alignment with our purpose in the world.

A powerful tool in practicing truth is listening to bodily feelings and emotions. Have you ever had a body sensation that told you a big no or yes, but you ignored it and later regretted not listening to that inner knowing? Our body is imbued with intuitive knowing. This is the wisdom of the enteric brain, located in our gut.

If you become still enough to listen—through the awareness practice, or through asana practice, or other movement therapies—you can begin to use your body as a compass to guide you along your path. Listening to our physical body helps us to cultivate trust in the body-mind connection, awakening the instinctive nature that many of us have lost connection with. This can be a bit confusing because sometimes we may feel big body responses for things that are fleeting, as in addiction, and other times we may feel a gut-level pull to do something, but the mind says no. When we are acting from surface desires, we mistake pain for pleasure and pleasure for pain. When we are balanced and not giving ourselves over to desires rooted in mistaken perception, we are prepared for a balanced response of body and mind.

Holding the intention of truth as a daily spiritual practice tethers us to the path of yoga, much as a leash and collar keep a dog on the path with its owner rather than wandering wherever its senses take it. The leash is short, but it doesn't strangle us because the path is leading us to greater knowing. Not doing what we say we will do—the seer-doer split—is what chokes us and causes us to suffer. We can start there. Keep your word to yourself. Next, keep your word to others. How many times do you find yourself inventing excuses about why you can't make an appointment when in fact the problem is that you have over-extended yourself? Simply tell the truth. Every day.

Practicing truth means remaining authentic to ourselves even in our relationships. When you lose connection with yourself, you are left with an emptiness inside that you then try to fill through connection with someone else. But reaching out to connect when we are empty can never actually satisfy us. Only when we are full inside can we truly connect with someone else.

Not only that. When we are empty inside, we have nothing to give to others. We are hasty with them. We don't give them the time, space, and listening that create a loving and safe environment. Haste is a form of violence and breeds more violence, as we can see in our culture and all around the world. Truth always creates a safe space, which is why truth and nonviolence go hand in hand.

Truth was the first yama I started to practice—without knowing it was a yama—and that practice eventually led me to yoga. While recovering from an eating disorder, I had realized that manipulation and lies were at the root of the suffering I was experiencing in my relationship with myself and with others—as they are for any addiction. I also saw that my efforts to always please others distorted my own authentic behavior, for when you are trying to be who you think others want you to be, you lose yourself and the truth of who you are. So I set the intention to practice truth.

Practicing truth helped me to say yes to all parts of myself. It helped me find the courage to ask questions about outcomes I was expecting and about my real agenda. Truth can be scary, because truth means accepting what is, and we may not like what we see.

Going against the grain of my tendency toward people pleasing meant I needed to approach relationships while remaining loyal to what was true to me. In fact, this became part of the way for me to learn who I really was. Although now people would not likely label me as introverted unless they knew me quite well, I was a self-proclaimed introvert, always avoiding social settings because, as a people pleaser, I would find myself acting out of alignment with my truth.

Therefore step one for me was to make a practice of saying yes to things to which my knee-jerk reaction was no, which was most things. (If you are an extrovert, a key practice for you may be to say no to certain situations and spend more quiet time in solitude, even if that sounds frightening.)

Step two was to show up fully as myself without worrying about what people thought of me. At first, I swung like a pendulum to the other extreme. I changed from repressing my truth to living and speaking my truth without apology. I was truthful to the point of violence. But just because I was clear about my perspective didn't mean it was the truth for others. Eventually I discovered that truthfulness and nonviolence (*satya* and *ahimsa*) must work together, like two strands of a rope that holds our attention to the path of service, devotion, and love.

Aligning with Truth

Begin incorporating truth into your life with the practice of keeping your word. Do not break the promises you make to yourself and others.

If you realize that the promises you make are setting unrealistic expectations, ask yourself why. This opens up another level of inquiry into truth. Are you trying to be someone other than who you are? Are you comparing yourself with others? Are you saying yes to please people, when you really want to say no?

Align with your personal truth by taking time to listen to your desires and journal about them. Are your desires coming from the lower mind—are they temporary and usually passing? Are they higher desires that have been nagging you to fulfill them, though you have been resisting? Are they repetitive desires that are actually attachments? Notice if you have any judgment around these desires. Can you simply observe them as an inner reflection of the outer work on values we discussed earlier?

Nonviolence

> *The attempt to achieve and maintain justice, or to undo or prevent injustice, is the one and only universal cause of violence.*
> – James Gilligan

Nonviolence can be defined as the radical acceptance of ourselves and of others. Its opposite, violence, is any attempt to act out of alignment with our truth or persuade others of our way of thinking. It is difficult enough to attend to our own moment-to-moment right actions. How can we possibly judge another's actions from an outsider's perspective?

Among yogis, nonviolence (*ahimsa*) is often practiced with regard to food. I was a vegan for more than three years. It was a step along the path of my evolution from bulimic and anorexic to foodie. Adhering to a set of strict rules about what was ethical to eat offered enough structure that made me feel in control, even as it helped me heal my relationship with food.

This is one way to practice nonviolence—on the very physical level of food and nourishment. But ahimsa can also be practiced in the way we communicate with others. During the three years I was a vegan, I went around preaching to others about veganism and why they should adhere to the same rules that were now important to me. I was speaking my truth, but, as I just mentioned, thankfully, I eventually realized that I was in fact being violent to others as I tried to persuade them to adopt my nonviolent lifestyle.

How we use our hands each day as we move through the world can also be a place to practice nonviolence. After practicing nonviolence in my own actions for some time, I began sharing the concept of nonviolence in our household with my two little girls. Each night I would give them a lavender back massage to help prepare them for sleep. They liked to do this for each other as well. Before the massage, we took a moment to pause, look at our hands, and say aloud, "I only use my hands for love." This became our daily practice of ahimsa together. It was simple and sweet.

Then one day, I was sitting at the dinner table with my daughters, having just purchased some free-range chicken from the local food co-op. We were eating with our hands, something I love to do, having adopted it from the South Indian culture. In yoga, it is taught that the hands are an extension of the heart, and eating this way provides the heart connection with our food that we had as babies nursing from our mother's breast.

I looked down at my hands and at my children's hands tearing the breast of the chicken away from the bone and heard our mantra, "I only use my hands for love." It was then that the split in my value system caused by consuming animals became apparent to me.

I share this not to try to convince you one way or another regarding what you eat, but to show how what we practice gradually moves deeper into our consciousness, from where it can change our thinking and behavior.

Our hands express our emotions, reaching out and striking when we are angry, or reaching out to embrace when we are loving. When we recognize our hands as representing our heart, we become more conscious of how we are reaching out into the world. We may place our hands on the earth a little more gently. Holding a piece of meat and tearing into it may no longer be part of what we choose to do. Or we may just greet one another with more awareness as our hands meet. Noticing our hands and all the actions they perform each day slows us down so we can remember to reach out in a way that offers love and support.

Take mindfulness into your hands. The symbolic hand gestures (*mudras*) used in yoga can hold our intentions. One of the common mudras in yoga is *anjali mudra*, the heart offering used in a salutation. Bringing the two palms together at the level of the heart is a sacred gesture of coming together with ourselves, where left and right, masculine and feminine greet one another in the dance of love. How we hold our hands suggests how we are focusing the mind and directing our attention. The more focused we become, the more clear and single-pointed our sight becomes, and we can commit even more fully to the practices of honesty and love.

Our presence—who we are being—can be peaceful or violent, welcoming or hurried. The presence of a soldier may be very different from the presence of a mother, and the mother's from a monk's. Nevertheless, when it comes to practicing ahimsa, we can all begin somewhere. A nonviolent presence is rooted in the highest truth. Think of the presence of Gandhi and of Mother Teresa as examples of truth and love in action.

> ### Observing Nonviolence
> Consider the word "nonviolence" and what it means to you. Perhaps it means eating a vegetarian diet or speaking lovingly to others and listening to them. Maybe it means carrying bugs you find in your home to the door and releasing them outside instead of squashing them. Perhaps it is offering kind words and deep listening without losing your cool.
>
> Practice the form of nonviolence you have chosen for thirty days. Even if you succeed at your chosen practice only some of the time, you are still on the path to cultivating an attitude of nonviolence.
>
> Journal about your experience.

The Inner Yamas

It is no measure of health to be well adjusted to a profoundly sick society.
  – Krishnamurti

Noncomparing

As the outer yamas of truth and nonviolence become more constant in us, the subtler, inner yamas—noncomparing, moderation, and nongrasping—begin to awaken as part of our attitude toward life.

The Sanskrit term for noncomparing, *asteya*, means literally nonstealing and is often translated that way. But to understand asteya as a yama that is working at a more subtle level, we need to trace its meaning back to *why* people steal.

People steal because they compare. They see that someone else has something they want, and they reach out to take it from them—whether overtly, as with physical objects, or in less visible ways, as with subtle qualities the person has that we covet.

Comparing is often based on imagined data, since we cannot know everything about the person with whom we are comparing ourselves. We see this in the culture of social media. We read little bits of information about someone posted there, fill in the blanks with imagined details, and then decide how we feel about our imagined construct of that person.

When we compare ourselves with others, we feel either less than or greater than them. Even saying "I should be grateful because I could have it worse, like that person," we are stealing the other person's happiness. How is this so? Comparing leads to pity—pitying either ourselves or the other person. Pity is the enemy of compassion. Pity is stealing someone's hope, whereas compassion is giving someone hope—even if only through a thought or prayer. Compassion is rooted in the recognition that we are all equal. When we are comparing ourselves with others, we are not coming from a place of equality.

> *When we stop comparing, we can begin serving in the way we are meant to.*

Comparison, whether in its overt or less seen form, is a way of telling the universe that we don't trust we will have enough. Therefore, it robs us of our own hope. One of the most important teachings of the Bhagavad Gita is that it is better to do our own duty (*dharma*) poorly than to do another's perfectly (18.47). We can miss our own path because we are worrying about what everybody else is, or is not, doing. This is the disconnect so many of us experience in modern culture. When we turn our attention to ourselves, we can begin to appreciate our own gifts and then develop them so we can eventually give to others through those gifts.

Giving is the opposite of stealing. When we stop comparing, we can begin serving in the way we are meant to. Knowing who we are and what we are here to do (*dharma*) is the power we need to reclaim, and it begins with asteya.

I learned about not comparing but instead trusting one's own dharma on two trips to India. On the first trip, in 2012, I visited the state of Kerala in South India with my asana teacher, Shiva Rea. The landscape of Kerala is tropical, like the Caribbean, and the society is matriarchal. The people are relaxed and fluid in their bodies. Being there is like being in the comforting arms of a mother. I was charmed by the people and the culture, and I could feel something happening deep in my navel, as if some deep issue were stewing.

One evening, I sat in meditation for an hour, not aware of time passing or the tears streaming down my face. Something was resolving deep within me—something feminine and fierce that would eventually heal my relationship with my mother, all the mothers who came before, and all those to come after. The next morning, I woke up in a state of clarity and heard a voice saying, "Do not be distracted."

I returned home to the States with a mind more clear and a presence more rooted in trust. From this deep resolve I experienced what seemed like a miraculous break from the conditioning of my lower mind and the distractions caused by a lifetime of comparing. I was now acting with greater authenticity, and forming my life from this place allowed me to give more. From this new, clearer state of mind, I was able to develop Sattva Vinyasa, the holistic style of yoga I teach, and our yoga therapy diploma programs.

On my second trip to India, the following year, I visited the sacred city of Varanasi. The two places could not be more different physically and culturally. In contrast with Kerala, the streets of Varanasi were crowded and noisy, and the skies were cold and gray. Even the shapes of people's bodies were different. Rather than the softly curved bodies I had seen in Kerala, the bodies of people in Varanasi were thin, strong, and almost triangular, with broad shoulders held high to their ears and narrow waists above steady, wraithlike legs. Their gaze was fierce, like a flame. When we thanked our guide for leading us, he replied, "It is my duty. This is my dharma!"

It was from the people of Varanasi that I began to understand how the practice of not comparing comes from a deep trust in one's dharma. The city seemed chaotic on the surface. However, when I peered into people's eyes, I saw soulful individuals acting out perfectly their God-given parts in the play of the world that appeared so imperfect. The sight of the beggars on Varanasi's streets—living amid the dirt, noise, and poverty—wounds a place inside the Western heart-mind, for Westerners are the problem solvers of the world.

We compare and we feel pity. We want to assert our power rather than surrender to simple virtues like faith and trust.

However, in the beggars' eyes, I saw a deep knowing and confidence that is rare in our culture of success. When I shifted my gaze to meet theirs, a spark and a smile, not unlike that of the Mona Lisa, came across their faces as if to say, "I know, I am." I then realized that I had seen the same kind of trust in the people of Kerala. It made possible their authenticity in relationships and the harmoniousness of their culture.

As I continued to practice not comparing myself with others, I stopped putting everyone and everything into categories, into boxes, labeling those boxes, and then judging those labels. At first, it was scary to break those boxes down, but soon it became exhilarating. By breaking free from the prison of comparison, I could commit all the more deeply to my own path. I then fell in love with yoga all over again because it was showing me how trapped I had been, losing sight of my authentic self.

Sometimes I am asked by society or by expectations associated with roles I play or simply because I am a woman, to crawl back into a labeled box. And sometimes I think about crawling back into one on my own, because it is easier to get what we expect from other people or to be who they expect us to be if we are boxed and labeled. Here is my response to that:

In trampling out all the negative thoughts I had about myself, I trampled out all the negative thoughts I had about you. In stomping on the judgments about who I was, I stomped on the judgments I had made about you. In learning to love myself, I started loving you.

You are my teacher, and I am yours. So let us not ask anything of each other. Just synchronize your breath with mine, and let's be here together, as we did when we were kids, not swayed by the judging mind, not trying to be someone other than who we are.

When we break down the walls we have built around ourselves to keep us safe, we break down the barriers we have built against each other. When we stop comparing ourselves with others, we stop looking outside ourselves for something to make us whole. Then we can rest more comfortably in ourselves.

> ## Practicing Noncomparing
> As you go through your day, notice every time you compare yourself with others. When you see yourself comparing, do not change it or resist it. Simply ask yourself what you would be doing if you weren't engaged in comparing. Comparison is the biggest thief of time. What would you rather be spending your time on? What makes you light up?

Moderation

The Sanskrit name of the yama I call moderation is *brahmacharya*. Brahmacharya means celibacy and is usually translated as such, but as an inner yama it also points to something more subtle. Especially for householders, it is useful to understand brahmacharya as moderation, meaning the appropriate use of the senses. That is, the yogi or seeker is able to direct the energy of the senses, when he or she chooses, to flow not outward after sense objects, but inward as vital energy, which is required for us to heal ourselves and to fulfill our life purpose.

> *When we break down the walls we have built around ourselves to keep us safe, we break down the barriers we have built against each other.*

To moderate the energy of the senses, we need to become aware of what the senses are doing. Often, it is obsessing about the next pleasurable thing. Obsessions can drive us to a state of imbalance. I recall hearing actor and film director Philip Seymour Hoffman say, in a documentary about his life and work, that there was nothing pleasurable he hadn't made himself sick on. I think this is true for many of us in this affluent culture. Think of helping yourself to an abundant buffet and, after eating, sitting at the table feeling miserable.

Hoffman also commented that our happiness is something other people talk about at our funeral, but we never get to experience it ourselves. This also has to do with not learning moderation. When we begin moderating the senses, we start to notice that eating all that food is not as satisfying as we imagined, that it is more satisfying to feel light but nourished than to feel miserable after eating.

> *Slowing down and pausing is one of the best ways to develop moderation.*

When we chase after sense cravings, we are chasing fool's gold. It feels attractive and important in the moment, but it doesn't lead us to the happiness we are really seeking. We think we are passionate creatures chasing after the next adventure, but really, we are running away from our purpose, which is the real adventure.

The Bhagavad Gita illustrates how we run after one desired experience after another, with the example of a chariot (the body) being pulled in all directions by five wild horses (the senses). We think we are headed to our chosen destination, but in reality, the senses are dragging us here and there. When the senses direct our choices, the lower mind is in charge. When the senses are moderated, the higher mind is guiding our choices. Allowing the higher mind to drive the chariot is one way to define yoga.

As we learn to stop leaking our energy, we have more genuine vitality and enthusiasm for living. We settle into the present moment. It is only when we are living in the present moment that we can unlock genuine pleasure and engage the full spectrum of sensory experiences, ranging from distaste to joy.

When I had an eating disorder, all of my mental, physical, and emotional energy went toward food and body image. It was the practice of moderation that flipped the switch for me. By reining in the senses, I was set free from the self-defeating binging and purging cycle. My relationship to food changed. I began to recognize its relationship to the nurturing life force, and I started enjoying cooking and being cooked for and savoring food. It is like this with any addiction. To reclaim the energy of our senses is to return to our place of power.

Slowing down and pausing is one of the best ways to develop moderation. Among all the life forms on the earth, humans are the only ones who rush through life. Rushing pulls us out of our center. When we slow down, we can notice what is actually going on both around us and inside us. But slowing down takes courage because it means owning the entirety of what we are experiencing, not just what is pleasing to us.

When we slow down and pause, we can start to listen. We all want to be heard, so begin by listening to yourself, as in the awareness practice. Listening is the most powerful tool we have to come into harmony with ourselves. This is not the listening we do with our ears but the internal listening we do when we get quiet enough to hear our bodies being filled with breath.

Listen to your body's subtle messages. The body is giving us messages all day—messages about pain and pleasure, anxiety and boredom, and all the experiences in between. Noticing these subtle body sensations, called interoception, allows us to make better choices about how we spend our time and whether we are nurturing or draining our vital energy. It is a skill we help students develop in yoga therapy to help them connect with their body's ingrained need for balanced self-care.

Listen to your body as if it were a compass. It will tell you what you need to nourish yourself in each moment—whether it be movement or rest, food or no food, or a change in your environment or the company you keep.

One late-fall morning, I was feeling agitated during an early morning writing session. My body was restless, and my mind was overactive. My body's intuitive message to me was to take a break, get outdoors, and run the trails around the park nearby. My lower mind responded, "No. It is November, a good time to snuggle inside and be a writer." My slightly higher mind chimed in, "I'm labeling myself: writer. The ego loves labels, but labels eventually become obstacles. When we label ourselves, we bury ourselves."

> *Listen to your body as if it were a compass.*

I decided to listen to my body's wisdom. Even though my lower mind offered a number of excuses—"Don't do it. It's been too long since you ran last. You have to conserve your energy for teaching yoga tonight. You don't want to be sore tomorrow."—I put on my running shoes and went out the door. There is a part of us that likes to give in to our fears or our preferences, that is waiting to devour our ability to be in the moment. This is never the part of ourselves we should trust. On the other hand, tuning in to the present moment without projecting expectations onto it aligns us with a greater truth.

After the run, I was clear, focused, and ready to sit down and enjoy writing, rather than fantasizing about being a writer. If I had not listened to that simple request from my body, I would have spent the afternoon eating extra food, drinking coffee, and trying to artificially create the clarity that the run gave me.

The awareness practice helps us cultivate the power of pause, so we can listen to ourselves. Another way to develop moderation is with a *pratyahara* practice. In pratyahara, the fifth limb of yoga, we direct our life energy inward instead of leaking it outward through the senses. Instead of chasing after a sense craving, we learn to let the craving pass through us. In that moment of pause, we are able to recognize that we do not need what we are craving. We stop identifying with the part of our personality that has the craving. We see that this too will pass.

Pratyahara is not about rejecting or avoiding desires, for repressed desires always push back. Instead, you can accept the desire and use it as kindling to ask questions such as "What do I really want in the long term?" "Is this use of my life force honoring that higher want?" You may not need to answer immediately. Simply digest the emotions you are feeling and let go of the story your lower mind has been making up. Invite your higher mind to drive the chariot.

When I first started meditating, I would become upset when I found that I couldn't still my mind. I kept trying. I stared at a candle. I counted my breaths. I felt the mala beads run through my fingers as I repeated the chant. Then one day, I gave up. I call this the great exhale of myself (*svaha*). I just let the chaotic dance of my mind be what it was. And I found peace.

I began to teach this as "the full-catastrophe meditation," as that is what it emerged from. Later, I learned from a teacher friend of mine that this is an *antar mauna* technique, a pratyahara practice of inner silence.

This antar mauna practice is a return to the awareness practice but takes the awareness to a deeper level. It is an opportunity to just sit with the sensations of the body, with the mind and all its reactions, with the emotions and any story you have created around them and watch it all come and go.

This practice can even help in dealing with pain. We sense pain as fixed and unchanging, but most pain sensations are actually variable. By simply sitting with the pain, not pushing it away, we can eventually notice its rising and falling and thus find moments of relative ease.

Pratyahara Practice: The Full-Catastrophe Meditation

Take a comfortable, supported seat as you do for the awareness and sitting practices. Notice your body and observe your breath for several cycles. As your body and mind slow down, start to notice what is happening in this moment.

Experience the sounds, the smells, the temperature of the air around you, the touch of whatever you are seated upon.

Allow anything that comes into your mind to be like a passing wave that has its beginning, peak, and end expression of the quality of itself.

Pause and see.

Notice everything happening around you as the great cacophony of the creative life force expressing itself, with you at the center. Like the center of a tornado. Just notice, with the wonder of a child.

Slowing down and using the power of the pause allows us the space to recognize that everything is holy. Whatever you are doing, you can do it as an offering, so it can feed your life energy rather than deplete it, so you can sit with contentment even in the midst of chaos and let go.

Nongrasping

Aparigraha, the innermost of the five yamas, is translated as nongrasping. We are all clinging to something—our ideas, our achievements, our beliefs, our loved ones. The lower mind wants to grasp every little thing and make it a big thing.

Grasping onto things and people makes us feel secure in our environments at work and at home, but that sense of security is ultimately false. We work hard at our jobs, but one day we will stop working and retire. We build a good resume, purchase a big house, raise an adorable family—and then what?

At work, we adorn our office or cubicle with objects and photos of the people we are working hard to provide for. Leaving an imprint of who we think we are in the space gives us a sense of security. Our altars hold images representing beliefs we are attached to. These rituals bring us peace and purpose, but yoga always prompts us to ask: And then what?

At a more subtle level, we collect moments of achievements and even mystical experiences just as we collect things. What are we collecting all of this for?

One afternoon my younger daughter, Teaghan, who was four at the time, and I were walking home from her school. She had been collecting rocks in her pocket along the way, and suddenly she realized the rocks were gone. They had somehow slipped out of her pocket. She fell dramatically to her knees, crying for fifteen minutes over the loss. Her tears were beyond my consoling. As I watched her going through this experience, I began wondering what rocks of my own would cause me to spill tears and lose myself in grief.

I am sure that God looks at us, entangled in our attachments and crying over our losses as if over a handful of lost rocks. It doesn't matter if it is a rock or a diamond. What are you attached to in an unhealthy way?

I had always considered myself a fairly nongrasping person when it came to expected outcomes of creative projects and relationships. A vivid dream one night revealed to me just how deeply I was grasping onto things.

In the dream, my family and I were at a couple's home for dinner when suddenly I felt an incredible urge to run. I instantly realized that *we were what was for dinner*. An energy force like a vacuum was about to devour us, so I grabbed my things, including a suitcase, and started running. I snatched up Teaghan, and as I noticed her sister, Brenna, standing in a darkened doorway, as in a scene in the movie *Poltergeist*, I grabbed her with my other arm.

The force was getting stronger, and with a child in each arm and all of the *stuff* I was trying to bring with me, it was becoming nearly impossible to move. I was stressed about the clothes falling out of my half-zipped suitcase, but still, I would not drop it. Then I turned to my partner and told him to go back into that voracious energy field to *grab my MacBook.*

Someone said that God speaks to us in whispers. Well, that isn't always the case. That dream was a slap-in-the-face lesson in nongrasping.

The next day, as I moved around my home, I noticed a bookshelf full of dusty yoga books (the kind you surround yourself with when you first begin to teach because they give you a confidence you don't believe you naturally possess) and a desk full of papers, notes, and bills from not one but two yoga studios. I glanced at my MacBook, the thing for which I had so willingly sent my partner back into the flesh-eating energy pit, its electronic desktop cluttered with icons of old yoga photos, flyers, links, and anatomy pictures. I began to wonder if this was a reflection of my mind—the thing I came to yoga to calm but had simply cluttered with new attachments.

If the spiritual path is all about letting go, why had I acquired so much stuff? I was attached to my MacBook, to Facebook, to yoga books, right alongside seeking liberation. The Vedanta scriptures say that even the desire for liberation is bondage.

Thankfully, when I stray off the path too far, God screams at me to get back on it and continue practicing. I began practicing letting go, packing a little lighter, as it were, so I could zip my suitcase completely.

Spiritual practice is always a matter of letting go, yet one of the pursuits in life, according to the Vedic tradition, is *kama*, the fulfillment of worldly desires, like accumulating wealth and power and embracing sex. This is part of our creativity and our role in continuing the human race, fulfilling our duty to create and care for family. The acts are often pleasurable and we enjoy pursuing them, but when we get caught in the pursuit we are no longer in the joy.

When we can appreciate our "rocks" with open hands and pockets, realizing that we are all just passing through, we give freedom not only to ourselves but to others. This doesn't mean giving up things or pushing them away. It means to love and care for them fully as long as they are in our care. We don't need to collect anything more than what we need to fulfill our duty, our dharma. We have nothing to gain or lose, for we leave the world exactly as we come into it.

When we hold on to people, we also set limitations on them rather than allowing them to move in the direction of their own dharma. We are meant to walk each other home, not lead each other astray.

Like all of the skillful behaviors, nongrasping takes courage, patience, and trust because it asks us to do something that most of us fear. To be okay with letting go we must first be okay with change.

We certainly cannot will ourselves to become nongrasping. Rather, doing the awareness practice, along with practicing the other skillful behaviors, tends to cultivate a natural faith that something greater than the things we want to grasp is holding us all—like a mother watching over her daughter as she cries over lost rocks, knowing this will pass. The more we trust that we are cared for, the easier it is to not hold too tightly to our pleasures, things, people, and experiences. Nongrasping opens the door to faith.

> *To be okay with letting go we must first be okay with change.*

Identifying Your Labels

Notice the labels you apply to yourself. Some of them are roles you play: mother, father, child, sibling, addict, friend, home owner, and so on. Some are ways you or others describe you mentally or emotionally or in terms of qualities: beautiful, sensitive, energetic, unhappy, depressed, and so on. These are all identities to which we have attached certain ideas and values. None of them are good or bad, but all of them, even the positive ones, subtly cover the strength and stability of who we are as a whole being.

> Write each of your labels on a Post-it Note or a note card, and spread the notes out on the floor.
>
> Now, following the sequence of the panchamaya model and the awareness practice, try this exercise:
>
> One by one, flip over any notes that you consider physical labels or roles you play. Notice your feelings as you turn over each one. Turning the notes over, so the words are hidden, loosens the grip those identities have on you.
>
> Then, one by one, flip over any notes that describe you energetically. Then flip over any that describe you mentally. Finally, turn over any that describe you emotionally. Again, as you turn over each note, notice your feelings.
>
> Are any notes left? Flip those over as well.
>
> Watch as all your notes gradually become blank. How do you feel about that?

This practice is not much different from a meditation in which we sit with the light within us, an impenetrable flame that is beyond the labels we wear. We remember that we are not the labels, that love is who we are. With this in our consciousness, we more easily conform to what the highest journey has in store for us, for love is behind everything we do.

Two Universal Sacred Practices

A new command I give you: Love one another. As I have loved you, so you must love one another.
 – John 13:34

Seeing the Light in Others

The word "yoga" means to join or yoke, whether the coming together is the joining of parts of ourselves, connecting with Spirit, or connecting with other people. TKV Desikachar, recognized as the father of yoga therapy, spoke about yoga as relationship. It is through our relationships that we can see the beauty that exists all around us, which is a stepping stone to discovering that we are all one.

To see the beauty in others, we begin by seeing beauty in ourselves. At our yoga institute, the words "You are beautiful" are painted on the front desk so people see them as they first enter. It is a reminder, an invitation, to suspend their assumptions and agendas for a moment and just appreciate their own beauty.

When we see beauty in the world around us, we are in awe of it. We look at the vast blue sky on a summer day and do not ask it to be different. We simply appreciate its beauty. We look at a mountain and do not ask it to be different. We simply appreciate its beauty because we have nothing to ask of it. We can do the same when looking at another person. Seeing the beauty in others is a step toward compassion, as it causes us to set aside our judgments and labels and just abide in the light we share together. When we make a practice of seeing the beauty, the light, in others, it becomes possible to see that light even in the worst circumstances.

We all want to be seen. To see ourselves, we can look in a mirror or at the surface of a calm lake, yet we see only a face and body that have been flipped into their opposite. But when someone else truly looks at us without story or agenda, he or she is seeing us from the healing space of "I am love." From this space of true connection, the other person helps us see ourselves for who we really are in a way not possible in the reversed imaging of a mirror. This kind of reflection back to us from another living being is the meaning of the Sanskrit word *namaste*.

Namaste literally means "salutations to you." The word carries a richer, deeper meaning in Indian and yogic culture—something closer to "the light in me bows to the light in you."

> *Seeing the beauty in others is a step toward compassion, as it causes us to set aside our judgments and labels and just abide in the light we share together.*

At the end of most yoga classes, the teacher leads the students in saying "namaste" while bringing their palms together with a bow of the head. It is easy to participate in this ritual without engaging its deeper meaning. At the end of the classes I teach, I invite everyone in the room to bring their palms together at their forehead. We bow and say "namaste" while looking into the eyes of everyone in the room. I invite everyone to really see the people they shared their practice with. At the end of class, everyone's face is a little more calm, their bodies more relaxed. They have a certain contentment. We gaze at one another without agenda, not needing to know each other's story and not stuck in our own.

In this prayer hands gesture, anjali mudra, we bring our right and left palms together, uniting the two hands which brings together the right and left hemispheres of the brain, yoking together the head and the heart. From this balanced place we salute the impenetrable flame of the heart that connects us all. The goodness that lives in all beings is waiting to be tapped by the simplest of kind gestures.

I learned the meaning of *namaste* from a fellow passenger on a plane ride. I was traveling from the Midwest to New York City in April 2013, shortly after the Boston Marathon bombing. After taking my seat on the plane, I watched as the other passengers came down the center aisle, stored their carry-ons, and took their seats. Nobody was smiling except one gentleman, whose smile was filled with much light. Serendipitously, he sat down in the seat next to mine. I acknowledged him with a smile and prepared to dive into some self-indulgent inspirational reading, but sometimes the best inspiration comes from experience, not a book.

He kept smiling, connecting, and seemed to see me deeply. Almost immediately, to my own surprise, I mentioned that I was into yoga. He sat back and said, "Okay, let me think of some questions for you." "Oh no!" said the slightly neurotic voice inside my head, "My random act of kindness has gotten me more involved than I want right now." But over the next two hours he proceeded to teach me by asking me to teach him.

Be careful what you ask for because you may receive it, and once it has arrived, you cannot fall back into your comfortable habits. Through a simple smile and eye contact, I had put a spark of light out into the universe on a dreary day full of heartbreak, and the Divine showed up next to me on the plane, giving back a thousand times more light.

At the beginning of our conversation, I was searching for something I should be wary of in this man—something that was dark—but all that existed was light and beauty. His essence was crystal clear. I wondered quietly: Why are we always on the lookout for darkness? Why do we insist that others prove they are good?

I was in disbelief that conversations like this really happen. Grasping for something tangible to ground me,

I started to talk about my business dreams and plans for the future. When the conversation shifted again as I began sharing my deepest spiritual ideas with this person I had just met and listening with an open heart to his, I think we were both speechless. As we prepared to deplane after reaching New York, we did not say goodbye. We just exchanged mala beads, his from Tibet and mine from India.

It is in such moments of experiencing Light through other humans that we recognize we are held by something much bigger than our own nature and will. Namaste is a practice that allows us to acknowledge the oneness connecting us to each other and all living things.

> ### Connecting with Your Heart
> In the morning, as you get ready for the day, take a minute to place your palms together at your heart center, with your thumbs gently meeting your sternum, and breathe into your chest. Perhaps you will feel your heart beating against your wrists or your thumbs.
>
> Connect to your breath and feel it deepen. Soften into yourself and bow your head slightly. Empty yourself and connect to the always pure, untouched space beyond drama, trauma, illness, and success or failure. Connect to the place beyond the physical, mental, emotional, and personality-centered places we witness during the awareness practice. Allow this connection to create an imprint for your day.

> As you go through the day, try to see others from this same place. Set a loving gaze upon the people you meet. See them beyond their surface personality with eyes of nonjudgment and understanding. Drop any agenda you may have. Let go of expectations. What is left? Your true nature meeting their true nature, light seeing light.

Forgiveness

Gathering resentments seems to be a natural part of living. Holding on to resentments never has a positive outcome. It puts a heavy load upon us. We may have freely given love and trust to someone, only to find that the person didn't live up to our expectations. Or someone may have hurt us out of his or her own karmic wounding, leaving us with a scar. If we keep reacting, living our life from this scar and the stories we have created about that situation, we continue the cycle of resentment.

As Johns Hopkins psychiatrist Karen Swartz says, "If someone is stuck in an angry state, what they're essentially doing is being in a state of adrenaline. And some of the negative health consequences of not forgiving or being stuck there are high blood pressure, anxiety, depression, not having a good immune response. You're constantly putting your energy somewhere else."[4]

If, instead, we apply the medicine of forgiveness to that scar as a daily practice, we clear up our attachment not only to what happened but also to the person who scarred us. Then we are free to move forward in life from a place of compassion and understanding. This is good for our minds and bodies. We can lay down the burden of our indignation and take our first steps lightened, as if with wings.

Forgiveness is about reconciling our relationships with not only others but also ourselves. For years, I was in denial about who or what I needed to forgive, perhaps because I knew unconsciously that it would mean taking a look at myself as well. At the beginning of a forgiveness practice, we identify the resentments we are carrying and the person we are resenting. We can also take a look at our own beliefs and whether those beliefs helped to allow that situation or person to hurt us. Perhaps the resentment we are carrying reinforces our belief that we are not enough or justifies how we treated someone.

If it is not someone else we need to forgive, then perhaps it's ourselves.

In my case, I realized I was holding on to resentments toward my mother. I was holding on to how she had made me feel about myself, as well as expectations about the outcomes of our interactions, which would then manifest just as I imagined. Once forgiveness graced our relationship, from years of practicing letting go of my resentments and saying I forgave her, everything about our interactions changed. I started looking forward to our time together and would leave after our visit feeling loved. I could look at the smile on her face and feel pure love. Was it she who had changed? Did we change simultaneously? Or was this the result of my setting the intention to let go of my resentments and forgive?

> *Forgiveness is about reconciling our relationships with not only others but also ourselves.*

The process of forgiving has many layers, and the deeper layers do not look like the ones at the surface. Once we are deep in the practice, we may begin to taste emotions that are the opposite of resentment. I found that the most beautiful gift of forgiving was a feeling of falling in love—that light, joyful feeling we have when we meet someone new or see our newborn baby. Forgiveness offers renewal and rebirth of the relationship between two people—or between ourselves and Spirit if we are forgiving ourselves. It creates a safe space for us to return home to.

Forgiveness is not something that we can will to happen. In cases of abuse, especially by someone who was supposed to be trustworthy, we may be able to do no more than hold space for the heartbreak of that relationship. However, with practice and grace, forgiveness can come. We don't have to carry the abuse, and we don't have to carry it on. The cycle of abuse can be stopped with forgiveness.

In his memoir, *Fire Under the Snow*, Tibetan Buddhist monk Palden Gyatso describes spending thirty-three years imprisoned and tortured by the Chinese with his brother monks. Though he was one of the oldest among them, he survived his younger healthier brothers. The secret to surviving, he writes, was to never let himself hold on to the hatred. While he was being abused he felt hatred, yes, but afterward he practiced looking at his abusers with compassion, realizing that their actions were due to their ignorance. Jesus taught the same thing from the Cross: "Father forgive them, for they know not what they do" (Luke 23:34).

A forgiveness practice is a powerful tool for releasing suffering. We can do this practice for ourselves, for a stranger, for someone who we know is suffering, for someone against whom we hold resentment, even for the world.

Forgiveness Practice

To prepare for this practice, first reflect upon the following questions or journal about them.
- Who or what do I need to forgive?
- Why has it been hard for me to forgive?
- Is it serving me in some way to keep carrying this burden?

- What do I believe will happen if I forgive this person?

To begin the meditation, sit upright on a chair with your feet firmly on the floor, or sit on the floor with your legs crossed and your sitting bones grounded on a cushion. Take a few moments to connect to your center and your breath.

Imagine yourself as the person you want to forgive, with his or her upbringing, beliefs, ideas, and life circumstances. Notice the struggles that might be taking place within that person. See his or her suffering and ignorance as a dark cloud blocking his or her light.

Create a safe space in your mind, and then visualize that person sitting across from you. Set aside any agenda you have about the person or about the relationship.

Imagine your heart as a brilliant light that disperses any darkness around this person or between the two of you. Feel yourself connected to the earth beneath you, safe and protected, as the darkness dissipates under the strength of your light.

Notice your breath: smooth, long, and full. Feel yourself soften as if the morning sun were gently shining on your face after a full night's sleep. A brand new day is awaiting you.

If the person you want to forgive has done or continues to do wicked things to you, yet you want to forgive him or her to free yourself from the burden of resentment, it is best to practice the forgiveness exercise while also keeping that person out of your life. However, if you realize the person appears wicked only because he or she has failed to live up to your expectations, practice the forgiveness exercise and also allow the person the space to be who he or she is. Begin to look for similarities between you, rather than focusing on the places where you go against each other's grain.

Medicines for the Mind: Healing Our Misperceptions

According to the yoga teachings, suffering has its source in a reactive state of mind. The reactive state of mind, in turn, is caused by false perception (*avidya*), which colors what we see and prevents us from seeing things as they are.

In Sutra 2.3, false perception is described as having four branches: ego (*asmita*), attachment (*raga*), aversion (*dvesha*), and fear (*abhinivesha*). These four tend to drive our actions when we are not acting with awareness.

In the course of doing my own practice and also working with students and clients, I have come up with antidotes, or "medicines," for these four misperceptions. By applying these medicines, we can move beyond the misperceptions and into the practice of yoga.

A Medicine for Ego: Stop Comparing and Start Listening

As mentioned earlier the ego is the part of us that loves to judge and compare, giving us a false sense of knowing our place in the world. It worries about keeping us safe from the judgments of our peers and it wants to protect us from the risk and vulnerability of being true to ourselves.

When thoughts of judgment and comparison appear, gently dismiss them. If you find yourself judging someone else, remind yourself that if you were that person, with his or her past memories and current desires, you would be acting exactly as he or she is acting. Remind yourself that you can never know the totality of that person's experience or the workings of his or her mind. Go inside your own mind and let the judgments go.

My yoga practice really began when I stopped comparing myself with everyone around me and started listening to the wisdom within me to guide me on my path. The best tools to develop inner listening are the higher concentration practices, such as breath practices, chanting, singing, and meditation. They hijack the busy, judgmental lower mind and cultivate the higher mind, which is more compassionate and can discern wise choices moment to moment.

A Medicine for Attachment: Let Go of Expectations

Attachment is having expectations for future pleasure, which sets us up for suffering. We want something today because we had it yesterday. We want what we do not have and want more of what we do have, but the spiritual path is always about letting go of expectations and replacing them with moment-to-moment right actions and a playful curiosity about life.

Attachment also creates haste, a level of overactivity that comes from surrounding ourselves with constant distractions because we are not able to find peace in being alone.

When you find yourself chasing after desires and wants, take a moment to slow down. Walk rather than run. Fast rather than eat. Give rather than take.

Breathing more deeply and softening our physical and mental response can help us let go of our attachments and let things flow in and out of our life, freeing us up to receive sweeter fruits. However, even those fruits are not ours to "eat"; they too are to be offered up.

A Medicine for Aversion: Imagine a New Story

Aversion is the voice of no that comes from self-doubt or from clinging to past experiences and projecting them into future ones. I am speaking here not about the voice of intuition that tells us no when it senses danger, but about the resistance that keeps us from stepping forward and saying yes to change. I have learned from experience that if my first reaction to something is a big no, that is a signal that I need to pause and think my reaction through. Most of the time, our response to life needs to be a yes.

Whatever is our reason for resisting doing the big thing on our bucket list is also what is blocking us from showing up fully in our day-to-day life. It's the part of you that convinces you not to move out of your comfort zone, to avoid doing the things that you have said really matter to you, like getting to yoga class, eating healthy foods, spending time with your family.

Resistance can be overcome through imagination. Often, when we say no, it is because we are replaying old negative stories and are afraid that we are going to get the same outcomes as before. Imagine a new story and a different outcome. Turn "no" into "now" and try something new.

A Medicine for Fear: Do Something That Scares You

In Sutra 2.3, Patanjali uses the word *abhinivesha*, referring to the fear of death. This fear, of course, is fear in its full-blown form—for instance, the fear that prevents you from jumping out of a plane. Fear in its less extreme forms is what prevents you from saying yes to opportunities and can cause you to suppress the natural urges of life, to stay in the safety of your comfort zone.

We can never overcome fear, but we can learn to deal with it and not let it stop us. Start by making a practice of doing things that scare you—not something that could put you in danger, but if you feel your heart beating a little faster at the idea of something that you know would mean growth for you, lean into doing it. Fritz Perls, the founder of Gestalt therapy, said, "Fear is excitement without the breath."[5] Breathe into moving outside your comfort zone. Color outside the lines. I dare you! Discover your inner child, who once knew that coloring outside the lines was okay.

> *The less we fear, the more we can enjoy life moment to moment.*

As you step out to meet this challenge, let go of whether you will succeed or fail. Often it is our fear of failure that keeps us from trying. I recently picked up the guitar again because I love to play. I get discouraged when I do not sound like Jimmie Hendrix (as I know I probably never will). When I am able to let go of needing to play perfectly, or even framing the experience in terms of success, I can simply enjoy making music.

The less we fear, the more we can enjoy life moment to moment. The more we practice letting go of attachment to success and failure, the more we can surrender and trust. And the more we surrender and trust, the more open we are to grace.

The Cracks Are Where the Light Gets In

When developing a practice of skilled behaviors, you may not always feel content. You will experience the tug of war between the lower mind and the higher mind. You will sometimes be caught in a cacophony of awareness, ignorance, and avoidance. As you become more aware of the disconnects between what you say and what you do, you will begin to notice the same in other people—and then decide they need to address their lack of inner truthfulness just as you are trying to address yours. This is a trap. As Ram Dass is said to have quipped, "I know I am enlightened because I can see how screwed up you are."

Nevertheless, as we wake up to our habitual patterns and pay attention to aligning our thoughts and actions with our values, other people experience us differently. Friends, partners, and coworkers will notice the change in us, possibly even before we notice it ourselves. They will notice that we are generally happier, more stable, and more at ease in the world. And they will feel more trust and safety around us.

In a yoga posture practice, the final posture, *shavasana* (corpse pose), invites us to let go completely. Our shoulders fall away from our ears, our hands let go of tension, our jaw relaxes, our eyes soften. When we relax into ourselves, we surrender to something bigger than ourselves. We are in a state where healing can happen, where God can get through.

Many of my students find shavasana to be the most challenging posture at first, but often it becomes their favorite posture. Over time, they learn to give themselves completely to the earth beneath them and let go of ego, attachments, aversions, and fears. The more we practice, the more we can place ourselves in the grace of something bigger than ourselves. Then our life becomes art.

A large part of our work is to stop grasping at the beautiful moments and pushing aside the painful ones, instead allowing ourselves to be fully present in all moments. Both beauty and suffering can break us open. As Leonard Cohen said, "There is a crack in everything, that's how the light gets in."[6]

May we bow with an open heart to all of life that has cracked us open. May we identify not so much with the cracks as with the light pouring in, illumining the way for ourselves and others.

STEP 3
SURRENDER

Initially, many of us are drawn to yoga practices because we are seeking power in some form: power over our thoughts, power over suffering, power over heartbreak, power over our work in the world. This desire for power is part of what motivates the seeker identity in us to engage in the practices of Step 2.

Yoga does offer access to power. It has to, being a path to enlightenment. To tap into our Light and to see clearly from there is the most powerful way to remove our own suffering and also help others remove theirs.

However, to tap into that Light and thus to experience the real transformation yoga offers, the seeker, ironically enough, has to at some point let go of the drive of seeking. This is a hard one for our egos to wrap themselves around, especially for seekers in this day and age. The attitude of entitlement that feeds the commercialism of modern culture has seeped into yoga culture as well. We have been conditioned to expect options—so we flit from one yoga tradition to another rather than going deep with just one. Or we assume we can become a teacher after six months of training rather than committing to yoga as a lifelong practice. So also, we may find ourselves approaching yoga as another thing to achieve—chasing after the bliss-filled moments of a spiritual high or wanting to get a yoga butt. Once we experience a moment of relief from suffering through yoga or meditation, we then want to re-create it. Even the desire to heal can become a form of seeking power over our body or emotions.

> *To the extent that we surrender to something so grand, we become a vessel for this Universal Will to flow through us and shape our actions in the world.*

This is where having no agenda (*vairagya*) is so crucial as the companion to practice (*abhyasa*). If we cultivate the attitude of agendalessness alongside the practice of skillful behaviors, then those practices lead us not down the deceptive, misleading path of seeking power but instead into the third step of kriya yoga, *Isvara pranidhana*, or surrender.

It was for this reason that my early yoga teachers warned me not to get caught up in the circus-trick aspects of yoga but to let go of attachment to the results of my practice. So when I see my own "type A" students striving through their practice to attain power over their bodies, other people, or situations, I try to offer the same guidance away from this ego trap and back to having no agenda.

The fact is, whatever power we may acquire always comes from a greater repository of power than ourselves. When we surrender to something bigger than ourselves, we ground ourselves in its gravity and grace. The longer we practice yoga and meditation, the more we understand this.

Initially, surrender can be to anything that you understand as bigger than yourself—for instance, to a certain yoga tradition or a trusted mentor. However, *Isvara pranidhana* literally means "surrender to God." Ultimately, all surrender is to that unchanging, formless form that is beyond our understanding.

To the extent that we surrender to something so grand, we become a vessel for this Universal Will to flow through us and shape our actions in the world. I like to call this Will power (with a capital W). In its ordinary sense, will power was something I—and perhaps you too—have lacked at one time or another. Constantly trying to will ourselves to be something other than ourselves. The little will can never be satisfied. Pausing to listen to a greater will and surrendering to it allows us to become a vessel for greater things to happen through us.

Sometimes we fall spontaneously into an experience of surrender. I had such an experience when I was in the fifth grade. I was best friends with a girl whose parents were "born again" Christians. We used to have sleepovers, listening to music, dancing, and eating ice cream. One evening during one of these sleepovers, my friend told me I should ask Jesus into my heart. I am sure now that her mother put her up to it, since I was her daughter's best friend and also a pop-culture-loving material girl.

I had no idea of Jesus at that point, as my parents never taught or talked about religion. I knew only the image of his face, full of compassion, that hung by my grandmother's door as I saw it every time I visited her home. So at my friend's invitation, I closed my eyes without understanding or conditioning and, in that moment, became a vessel of light. I felt the whole of my body illuminated by light, the way the rising sun illuminates a landscape. It was a gentle white light, and there was a warmth, like being in a mother's womb. I can't remember what happened next, and the more I try to speak of this mystical experience the further away it becomes. I don't remember if I was cradled softly to sleep or if I told my friend about my experience.

I believe we all are light, and that most, if not all, of us have spontaneous experiences like this at some point—signs that our spiritual sensors are working. However, yoga offers us a path, through cultivating skillful behaviors and an attitude of agendalessness, that naturally brings us to surrender.

rendered. I'm not sure how long I sat there, but it was much longer than a typical mediation, yet everything seemed to get done that day.

Another moment of surrender came while I was driving to a yoga therapy training. I had been suffering with a hip injury, and I was thinking about all of the techniques I could use to heal it. Suddenly, at a stop sign, I felt a force pushing into my chest, softening me back into my seat and myself, with the message: "Let me work on you." We are always busy working on ourselves. When we surrender to something bigger than ourselves, we allow it to work on us.

I sometimes ask my "achiever" students: "If you were in the middle of running a race and someone told you there was nothing to win, no finish line, what would you do? Would you say 'This sucks' and slow down or give up? Would you blame the messenger? Would you ignore the messenger and pretend there really is a race? Or would you surrender to the circumstances and say, 'If this is your will for me, Lord, I will keep running with all my heart'?"

The state of surrender is accompanied by a kinesthetic experience of "yes." From that yes, we become a vessel for our purpose—our dharma. Our dharma is truth forming our actions in the world, and also our actions forming truth. We become cooperators with God.

Surrender brings a greater level of ease. As we settle more deeply into the present moment and into ourselves, we find we are seated comfortably in ourselves. From here, we can explore remaining in that easeful state even while engaging in our practices and in our dharma. It is also in surrender that the parasympathetic nervous system is most easily accessed, which promotes healing.

Discovering Surrender by Letting Go

Jump and build your wings on the way down.
– Ray Bradbury

Getting to surrender is not always comfortable. One way to discover a doorway to surrender is by taking the opposite or contrasting view (*pratipaksha bhavana*).

One morning when I was sitting in meditation, I felt my whole body contract as thoughts of all the activities on my to-do list for that day flitted through my mind. Some were have-tos, and some were want-tos. Finally, I heard my slightly higher mind say, with a touch of sarcasm, "So you think you are doing something." Then my higher, wiser mind said, "It is all done in God." I felt my whole body go into a relaxation response. I landed in my asana, my comfortable seat within myself. I sur-

I first experienced this kind of alignment with a greater will in an Anusara yoga class in 2007, not long after living through a tumultuous life lesson on relationships. I was lying on the floor in a deep corpse pose (*shavasana*) after repeating the mantra *om namah shivaya*. For the first time in my adult life, I recognized God as a presence living within me tasting the experiences of life right alongside me, rather than as a wish granter dwelling outside me. I also recognized that when I am not living my values, I am causing a split between myself and the Divine. I saw that I can choose to align with truth and thus become a vessel through which a force bigger than my ego can stream through my life. In that moment, my human nature was reconciled with Spirit, leaving aside the struggle of whether I was good or bad, saint or sinner.

Discovering surrender inevitably involves the ego loosening its grip on what it wants and how it wants things to be. The Austrian poet and novelist Rainer Maria Rilke said, "Love and death are the great gifts that are given to us; mostly they are passed on unopened."[7] The ego, clinging stubbornly to its agenda, tends to resist its own "death" out of fear and to resist love because it might mean having to forgive. Yet the ego must die, that is, surrender, so we can rest in our true nature. The ego has to be broken open so that, in the process of putting ourselves back together, we call on a power outside ourselves. We can choose surrender. In aligning with a Higher Power, we open ourselves up to engaging in selfless service that comes from knowing "I am love."

Life gives us opportunities to let our egos be cracked open in this way. One such lesson I'll never forget happened when my grandfather was passing away from cancer in February 2012. I was on my way to lead a yoga retreat in Costa Rica and made a stop in Wisconsin to visit him before I left. There was a blizzard and I was rushing to his house, thinking that the two family members doing the caregiving were hardly qualified to guide him during this transition, being atheist and male. Could they offer the necessary emotional support and guidance as he passed from this body to something greater?

Opening the door and rushing into the house, I ran right into a wall of energy so intense that it stopped me in my snowy tracks and took my breath away. It seemed to be saying, "Do not interrupt the majesty that is going on here."

Usually when something stops us like that, it is an obstacle—dense, *tamasic* (inert, inactive, heavy). But this was a light force such as you feel when you walk into a cathedral. My two male atheist relatives had created what felt to me like a sacred temple for my grandfather's passing. They had come in simply as loving, open human beings, acting out of natural selflessness and without attachment.

The only obstacle in this scenario was my ego, my belief that some of us are limited in the amount of love we can give and that, as a yoga therapist and spiritual seeker, I could give more. I also stumbled right into two of my prejudices that had been hidden from me until that moment: that women are better caregivers than men, and that only people who believe in God can love someone through the dying process. As I bumped into the truth, my ego surrendered and I was able to witness the beauty that was present.

> *Everyone has the capacity to love beyond the expectations others place upon them, or even that they place upon themselves.*

Everyone has the capacity to love beyond the expectations others place upon them, or even that they place upon themselves. It simply takes their seeing someone in front of them to love and serve, and the illusion of limitation falls away. Just as we should not compare the shapes of our yoga postures, we should not compare the brightness of our souls.

We are all spiritual seekers in the end, though our paths are as differently shaped as the bones in our bodies. A wise man once said, "Once I became enlightened, I never met another person who wasn't."

Flow and Its Opposite

> *Then he said, "Come no closer! Remove the sandals from your feet, for the place on which you are standing is holy ground."*
> – Exodus 3:5

When we are able to let go and trust in a Will that is greater than our own, allowing that Will to flow through us and into our actions, we can fall into a state of flow. Flow is the state we experience in a moment of appreciating something beautiful, a moment that makes us respond with awe. This is where the writer becomes the story, the artist becomes the painting, the runner becomes the run, and lovers become love.

We have all experienced the spontaneous joy of flow at some time, to some degree. So also, we have all experienced its opposite. This is the changeability that is life. The state of flow eventually dissipates, and once again we feel confused as to who we are and what we are supposed to do.

The Ayurvedic principle "as is the macrocosm, so is the microcosm" reminds us that just as the seasons rotate and day turns into night, which becomes day again, so we too are meant to contract and expand. When we are at the peak of our creative energy, we feel alive, but this will fall again. What we "knew" a moment ago becomes irrelevant, a cloudy memory, as we get caught up in the next task.

As the contraction pulls us out of our flow, we may try to cling to that state or recreate it, searching for the next sunset, melody, or lover that will bring us to that place again. But that is not the point. You are sure to rise and fall like the waves of the ocean.

Life is a dance between dropping to our knees and getting back up on our feet, as in a sun salutation during asana practice. It is all the postures linked together, along with our awareness, intention, and breath, that make it a salutation, an offering.

To ride these waves comfortably—to enjoy the flow state when it arises and also find peace and comfort in the fall—involves discernment, a function of the higher mind (*buddhi*). As you are rising, remember where you come from. As you fall, take comfort in the support beneath you. When we let go of our preferences, realizing that everything comes from the same source, our whole life becomes a reflection of trust and surrender.

All of this becomes sacred if we remember there is a power greater than ourselves. Just as God called Moses's attention with the burning bush and handed Moses his purpose, so God calls us to our own purpose. Even if we do not fulfill our purpose perfectly, it is still our own, and the falling in and out of grace itself is a sacred state of flow.

One of my favorite Sanskrit words is *svaha*. *Sva* means "self," and *ha* is the exhale. We exhale ourselves into the expression of God through our life purpose in this moment. I like to think of this as "I exhale (empty) myself" or "I live in the exhale (service) of he who is Love."

> ### Practicing Surrender
>
> Start your day with five or ten minutes of sitting with the greater good, your Higher Power, or with the thought of something bigger than yourself and your mind. Set the intention to empty yourself for the sake of that greater good.
>
> If your mind starts running with thoughts of doing, or with fantasy or boredom, simply notice and bring your attention back to feeling yourself wrapped in the presence of perfection. All the thoughts, the ups and downs, the wanting to be better, and the selfish, dark thoughts belong and continue to move through your mind to that which holds them all.
>
> If you need something to anchor to, think of the mantra *svaha*, "I offer myself."
>
> Notice how the tone of your day changes on the days you do this practice compared with the tone of those days when you start your day running. Notice the difference that just ten minutes a day of surrender can make.

Beyond Flow and Nonflow

The very nature of creation is duality—life and death, growth and decay. The lower mind (*manas*) tends to react to the dualities with likes and dislikes—to choose one option and reject its opposite. It likes to desire and be repulsed, compare and measure, divide and conquer. The higher mind, or intellect (*buddhi*), with its capacity to discern, is able to look beyond the dualities to glimpse our true nature that lies beyond it.

In terms of the panchamaya model, described in Step 1, the higher mind (*buddhi*) is the vijnanamaya kosha. When the higher mind is awake and discerning, it naturally aligns with the still more subtle level of ourselves: the bliss body (*anandamaya*). Intuition is the bringing of spirit or bliss into thought (*buddhi*), from where it can shine through our actions at the physical level. This alignment of bodies fosters the state of surrender.

People who can access the perspective of the higher mind tend to develop the art of surrendering to both flow and its opposite. Do you sometimes find yourself in awe of people who seem to be genuinely happy, satisfied in their work and in their relationships? They are grounded and graceful, and not much seems to rattle them. They have reined in the senses and the lower mind enough to not take it all too seriously. We may be in awe of them—but that way of living is available to any of us who cultivate discernment.

We can find happiness in both success and failure, in both the rising and the falling of life, in both flow and its absence, when we trust in something greater that is holding them both. Some of my most blissful experiences have occurred during moments that were the most unhappy superficially, because those experiences forced me to reach for something deeper.

I stumbled unknowingly into a glimpse of this truth at an early age. When I was five years old, my parents decided to divorce. I remember them sitting together on the couch asking me to choose which of them I would like to live with. As I look back on the memory, I see it through the eyes of experience and understanding. They were in their early twenties, bitter with each other, but they loved me and wanted me to be where I desired. But for the child I was then, the power to decide between mother and father stunned me. I was caught in the pause, in the web of a mind that couldn't comprehend. Then the fear of breaking the heart of one of my parents crept in. I realized I could hurt someone with my power of choice. So instead, I began to twirl around in my white dress, curls bouncing up and down, as the sun twinkled between the two of them silhouetted on the couch in front of the

> *Trust in the joy (*ananda*) that is at the core of your being.*

picture window. That moment felt like eternity. I am not sure what happened after that. I just danced.

Go deeper than your thoughts and emotions, whether they are happy or sad, content or worried, and uncover the joy residing there. From that place, embrace the entire experience of being human: the light and dark, the good and bad, the success and failure. Trust in the joy (*ananda*) that is at the core of your being.

From that place, we see that we do not have to be disappointed by failures or attached to successes, for both are temporary. We do not have to be overwhelmed by an abundance of work or bored by excess time on our hands; we can embrace both. We need not be constricted by relationships to others or attached to fixing them. Instead, we can allow the intimacy and vulnerability of relationships to transform us.

Beyond Spirit and Matter

In Western culture, spirit and matter, spirituality and the world, are seen as mutually exclusive. The idea of something existing beyond duality is radical and rare. A person, also, is seen as both spiritual and human in nature, these two parts being difficult to reconcile. In this simplistic view, we then either turn our backs on God and become immersed in the material world or view the world as evil and God as the only thing that can set us free.

Feeling obliged to make this choice between our human selves and our spiritual selves precipitates suffering. We don't understand the cause of this suffering, so we numb ourselves with a profusion of choices. In this land of plenty, it is easy to become overwhelmed by the hundreds of choices before us—brands of deodorant and dishwashing liquid, diets to follow, reality TV shows to watch. As my teacher David Frawley described it, "The consumer is consumed."

The great paradox is that, in each of us, spirit and humanness are inextricably entangled. We can't choose one and deny the other without denying part of ourselves.

According to the yoga tradition, spirit and matter are not opposites or mutually exclusive. As the panchamaya model explains, spirit and matter are just different levels of reality. The way out of the trap of either-or, dualistic thinking is through awareness and curiosity, which are the medicines for all mental afflictions.

I once had a dream in which there were three beings: a male and a female who were speaking a language I did not understand, and a witness being who could understand their words and also experienced everything that both of them were sensing. Unlike in most dreams, I had no sense of ego, of being a single entity, in the dream; I identified with all three beings and with none of them at the same time.

In the dream, the woman was mourning the loss of someone or something she loved, even as she was dancing in freedom. The man, who appeared older and wiser, was watching her, desiring to be united with her. She was shy at first, but eventually she surrendered her shyness. They engaged with each other in a way that did not entangle them but was an interweaving of the two that set them free. I could feel the desire between the couple, though it was not mine. The witness also had no preference regarding the couple's choices; it was pure, agendaless awareness, held by a Will bigger than either of their wills.

When I woke from the dream, it took me a moment to get back into my body. Every human emotion flowed through me. Tears were streaming down my face, and when I could catch my breath I rolled over to face my partner and said, "I think this is what God feels like."

The dream powerfully illustrated for me that the key to reconciling God and the material world is to access the witness state of the higher mind, which watches the dance of life without agenda. To do this, we must choose what is beyond the black-or-white dualism that is how the lower mind is conditioned to see.

We are spirit and humanness entangled together. Spirit has preferences for what will fulfill our life purpose. The body has preferences for how it wants to fulfill the desires of the senses. Our role is to discover and live as best we can from the space between these choices. When we dance in this space, our dharma and purpose can flow through us.

Beyond Seeker and Sought

There is another duality we live with that's so close to us, we barely notice it. It's the duality between who we are as seekers and the truth we seek. This duality can resolve in the brief moments of mystical experience or absorption and awe that Patanjali calls *samadhi*. Whether it happens through surrender of the ego or by means of another practice, such as pulling the weeds of ignorance (*avidya*) or focusing the mind intently in meditation, when you arrive into a mystical experience, you arrive in the middle of God, the center of love.

Suddenly, the power you thought you had to seek becomes the power that is holding you. When we reach this state, if just for a moment, we experience ourselves as whole. Instead of the excitement of the pursuit of power, we land inside it. We become that which we are seeking. We realize that what we have been seeking is nothing but ourselves, that we are both seeker and sought. As the mystic Rumi proclaimed, "What you seek is seeking you."[8] With this insight, the persistent conclusion "I need love" shifts, remodeling itself into "I am love."

Another way to describe this experience: the seer becomes the seen. As Yoga Sutra 1.3 says, the seer abides in itself, rests in its true nature.

In this state, we perceive ourselves as whole and as part of the whole, rather than alone fighting against the world. This is like the shift that happens for Arjuna in the course of the Bhagavad Gita. At the beginning, he asks Krishna to drive his chariot out into the no-man's-land between the two armies gathered on the battlefield at Kurukshetra, where they stand alone. By the end of the Gita, he understands that he is not separate from everything. From this place of enlightenment, he is able to carry out his dharma, which in his case, as a warrior, involves fighting—but from a place of "I am love."

Observing the Breath inside the Breath

Sit quietly and simply observe your breath. Witness the breath move down to the belly on the inhale and then flow back up and out through the nostrils on the exhale.

After a few moments of following the breath, notice how the inhale creates space and fullness and the exhale creates grounding.

Now start to become aware of the turning points—at the top of the breath where the inhale turns to an exhale, and at the bottom of the breath where the exhale turns to an inhale.

> At the top of the inhale, notice the fullness of the breath. Reflect on your relationship to abundance in your life. At the bottom of the exhale, notice the emptiness of the breath. Reflect on your relationship to emptiness in your life.
>
> Sit with this awareness of your breath until you see all four parts of the breath—the inhale, the top of the inhale, the exhale, and bottom of the exhale, evenly, without preference. Abundance and emptiness, life and death, held together as one.
>
> The breath can be a great tool for sitting with surrender, which is why it is often used in preparation for meditation. What are you noticing during this breath practice? How comfortable are you at the two ends of the breath? The breath practice is ultimately about learning to give up control of the breath, to allow ourselves to be breathed. We don't have to think about breathing in order to breathe. The autonomic nervous system takes care of it for us. We don't "take" a breath. It is given to us.
>
> What is your relationship to the experience of letting go of control and simply noticing yourself being breathed?

Think of the breathtaking moments in your life. Perhaps the moment of orgasm. The moment a child is born. The first moment your eyes met the eyes of your future lover across the room. The moments spent gazing at the beauty of nature. The moment you lose someone you love. The moments when you realize you have lost yourself. These are the moments when our ego is cracked open enough that life can flow through, allowing us to see in a new light.

To live is to dance in the space between our first inhale as God exhales us out and our last exhale as God breathes us back in.

Compassion

If we have no peace, it is because we have forgotten to love one another.
 – Mother Teresa

When people engaged in some aspect of Step 3 take action in the world—whether theirs is a simple surrender to a greater will, the discernment that accepts and sees beyond the pairs of opposites, or a glimpse of mystical experience—their actions are likely to be different. The message they put out into the world shifts from "I need love" to "I am love." The natural next step is to want to give that love to others. The practice in Step 2 of seeing the light in others matures, here in Step 3, into compassion. Living from a place of surrender, they become the hands and feet of God acting in the world.

When I was in my early twenties, I wanted to be a compassionate person, but I found compassion exhausting to put into practice. I was working in a nursing home, and I would become attached to the people in the home, but then seeing them die would drain me emotionally. I realize now that, while my actions may have looked compassionate from the outside, I was merely imitating compassion. I have always been an empath. It is easy for me to weave with and feel the emotions of another. But compassion is different from empathy.

Empathy is taking on other people's shit. It is carrying them and their story with you. It is shape-shifting yourself into someone other than who you are for someone else's sake. Yoga therapists are advised to beware of "compassion fatigue" and burnout, but it is actually empathy, not compassion, that burns us out.

Compassion means literally to be "with passion." It also means to be with patience, since "passion" and "patience" come from the same Latin word *pati*, to suffer. I love the paradox of these two words placed together, because often we think of patience as calm and detached, and passion as active and engaged, like rushing into a lover's arms.

Compassion is not a feeling; it is an action. It is taking action to transform another's pain, but it is accompanied by dispassion, which is another form of having no agenda. It is dispassion toward their suffering, which means not taking on their story, as well as not projecting our story about their suffering onto them. Compassion also means having no agenda about the results of our actions—letting the results of the good works we do to help others roll off us like water off a leaf.

Compassion is also the ability to be a safe space for someone else in their most vulnerable moments. In my work

> *Compassion is not a feeling; it is an action.*

as a birthing doula, I sometimes post a "do not disturb" sign on the door so the medical staff won't interrupt the mother's deep process if it's not necessary. Similarly, sitting with someone in compassion is the work of not disturbing, of being simply a witness.

When we can be a truly safe space for others. In a state of compassion, the senses are awake and caring fully. We use all the senses to look care-fully, touch care-fully, listen care-fully, speak care-fully. We allow our hearts to break open with theirs, so the light can shine through both of us.

Many yogis are into the raw movement—they like raw foods. So also, yogis develop the capacity to accept raw emotion. At the beginning of our practice, in Step 1, we learn to see and then sit with the discomfort of our own suffering. With the compassion that is a natural part of Step 3, we discover the capacity to sit with others in their suffering, showing up in our natural state unmasked and fearless.

Make your heart a blank page on which others can express themselves without your intervening. Then walk away with your heart a blank page again. The moment you think "I helped that person," you have taken on their stuff. That is empathy, which is entangling. When you are in compassion, the other person can color all over you, but you remain a blank page.

Compassion defined this way has a certain fierceness to it. To witness someone in their most vulnerable moments without turning off your own authentic emotions and vulnerability takes courage. A compassionate heart is a warrior's heart.

As the fearlessness of compassion washes over us, we wake up. It is like your beloved pulling the covers away at dawn because he or she can't stand for you to sleep another minute of the day away. It is the energy of running naked into the street, as St. Francis of Assisi did, shouting, "I am alive and awake."

The Tibetan Buddhist tonglen meditation is a process of transforming the suffering of others without taking it on. You take on their suffering for a moment, but it is transformed by your compassion and returned to both of you as greater joy. The other person doesn't need to be physically present when you do this practice. In fact, it is better if he or she is not.

Tonglen Meditation

Find a comfortable seated position. Take a few moments to feel the support of the ground beneath you. Connect to the rhythm of your breath. After ten breaths, bring to mind someone who is suffering or whom you are worried about. Focus on any strong emotion you are feeling connected with the person's suffering.

Imagine that emotion or suffering as a dark cloud inside the person. On an inhale, pull this darkness into your own being, seeing it dissolving in the light of your heart. Breathe and feel your light. On an exhale, send that light to the other person. Imagine his or her face becoming brighter. Visualize the two of you seated together at peace.

The aim of yoga is to become seated comfortably in ourselves. We rest comfortably in ourselves when our choices are aligned with wisdom and discernment of the higher mind, and thus with the more subtle levels of intuition and joy.

As we become familiar with this space, we gradually develop the skill to remain seated comfortably in ourselves even in difficult times. We learn to move ourselves from suffering (*duhkha*) to happiness (*sukha*) regardless of the dance going on around us.

THE FOURTH PHASE
INTEGRATION

After traversing through the three steps of kriya yoga—awareness, embodiment or practice, and surrender—what happens next? We return to Step 1, awareness, and begin again. Although the three steps of kriya yoga are sequential and build upon each other, they are also cyclical. So we start over, but with greater understanding and faith. Our awareness is more clear. Our practices are deeper. Our moments of surrender are deeper and more clear. We recommit. This renewed commitment is what Patanjali is referring to when he says in Yoga Sutra 1.14 that yoga practice should be done over a long period of time, without interruption, and with full enthusiasm.

However, after Step 3 and before returning to Step 1, there is a moment of integration (*samyoga*). This moment is not unlike pausing and taking a breath in mountain pose (*tadasana*) before beginning another cycle of yoga postures in the sun salutation sequence. It is also similar to standing on a mountaintop after the long hike up. At the top of the mountain there's not much space. Our movements are constricted, and we don't stay there for long. But while we are there, our perspective is broad and far-seeing. So also, in the moment of integration, our options have become one-pointed (*ekagrata*), and we can see clearly what we are committed to. Everything extraneous–the lower mind and its divisiveness—falls away.

This moment of integration is not one of the three steps of kriya yoga. It's the space beyond, similar to the sound of silence that follows the mantra *om*, used in contemplation of ultimate reality. According to the Vedic tradition, *om* has four parts. The *o* can be broken into *a* plus *u*, because in Sanskrit grammar an *a* followed by a *u* becomes *o*. So, the first three parts of *om* are the sounds *a*, *u*, and *m*. The *a* is grounding. The *u* is awakening or empowering. The *m* is the state of flow. The fourth part is the silence into which the *om* merges at the end and from which the next *om* begins again.

The moment of integration and ease is also a moment of insight (*drishti*, meaning "sight" in both the physical and the intellectual or wisdom sense). Our capacity for sight, and insight, grows and matures, shifting from more physical to more subtle as we proceed on the yoga path. I see this with yoga students and yoga therapy clients even in their asana practice. Beginning yogis are often unsure of how to position their body in space. Their sight is directed outward, looking around the class to copy what others are doing and also looking at their own body at the physical level only—okay, here is where I put my foot, my arm.

After they have been practicing for a while, they can close their eyes during the vinyasa flows and look within. They might place their focus on their navel or big toe to help embody the postures. Their proprioceptive sense—the kinesthetic/neurological awareness that tells us where we are in space—deepens. They also start to witness the movement of their breath and mind. As they begin to experience the alignment of breath and energy with the postures, they start to notice their emotions, for breath is connected to emotions. Then a lot of emotional unpacking begins.

As their asana practice evolves further, so does their power of sight. Wherever they set their gaze, their body now moves into position accordingly. This alignment of body with sight spills into life—they start to notice how, by aligning vision and intention with values and Higher Power, one's life moves into position accordingly. Their gaze can be purpose-filled and fierce with creative energy even as it is as agendaless and innocent as the gaze of a newborn.

As we begin again with Step 1, we bring this new level of clarity into our awareness practice, our embodiment of the practices of the yoga path, and our surrender to a greater power. Each time we cycle through the three steps, we gain more clarity and skill—just as in asana practice there may be a pose that we don't like or that leaves us feeling discouraged, but as we continue to practice the pose, we eventually surrender to it. Then the pose works through us. It may even become our favorite. Just as children may at first push aside the vegetables on their plate, but over time they come to like the taste, and eventually they even ask for them.

In this sense, this book, as a guide through the three steps, is designed to be read and reread.

We move through the steps sequentially, the way the spokes of a wheel follow each other as the wheel moves forward. Yet all three Steps are also in play in every moment. Awareness is a deep listening to ourselves, from which flow our actions in the world. Surrender allows us to choose right, or dharmic, action. At the center of the wheel is where we can pause from time to time in samyoga, a breath of integration and clarity of focus.

As we recommit to cycle again through the three steps, we also recommit to allowing the Divine to work through us. Yoga is the art of perfecting relationships, including our relationship with the Divine. "Perfecting" is an ongoing process, not ever reaching an illusive perfection but always on the path toward increased unification. As we integrate the message that we are love, we gain insight about our relationship with the Divine.

Then God's love is no longer "out of sight" for us. This connection with the Divine supports every other relationship in our life and allows us to see more clearly the thread that connects it all. This is the path of joy.

Chanting Practice

Chanting is a wonderful way to remove obstacles and to nourish our relationship with our higher mind. The following ancient Vedic prayer can be chanted in Sanskrit or just spoken as a prayer in English.

Om asato maa sad gamaya
Tamaso maa jyothir gamaya
Mrtyor maa amrtam gamaya
Om shaantih shaantih shaantih

Translation:
Om, lead us from the unreal to the real,
Lead us from darkness and ignorance into light,
Lead us from the fear of death to knowledge of immortality.
Om, peace, peace, peace.

ACKNOWLEDGMENTS

This book emerged into form through the divine inspiration of the Pranayoga community. After teaching a yoga class or training, or after a yoga therapy session, I would often sit and reflect upon the magic that had just happened, and insights would come. Or a student might ask a question that would cause a pouring forth of this yoga teaching. I am always surprised that the more I teach and talk about yoga, the more energized I become. Thank you to my students for their breath that fills the space.

I am grateful for my relationships with all of my teachers. Nikki Myers and Marsha Pappas birthed me into the world of yoga teaching through their 500 hours of guidance. I have been studying with and assisting my teacher Shiva Rea since 2009, as well as studying with Richard Freeman and Robert Thurman. They and their teaching sustained me as I began a yoga community and teaching teachers. Jnani Chapman introduced me to the path of yoga therapy and service for others. It was her passion, compassion, and guidance as a friend and mentor for a decade before she passed that brought the true gem of yoga into my heart.

Carolyn Bond has been so much more than my editor. Carolyn birthed this book alongside me, helping me bring the inspired teachings into the bones and flesh of a book we can hold on to and embody.

Natascha Bohmann, a student of mine and also a brilliant copyeditor, perused each word, helping to give the text clarity while keeping my voice.

Katie Brown, who designed the book cover and interior, has accompanied me through all my entrepreneurial hungers and heartbreaks. Her enthusiasm is as refreshing as her graphics.

My students who have entered into an authentic therapeutic relationship with me and become teachers to me—this book couldn't have been developed without them. My thanks go to Chris, who told me, "You have to become a writer" at a time when I couldn't wrap my head around the idea of a book coming through me.

My gratitude goes to my husband, Greg, who has been a teacher to me of steadfast love.

My daughters, Brenna and Teaghan, have helped me bring these teachings to life by giving me a voice. It was when I became mother to them that I understood how to be a teacher of Love.

NOTES

1. T. S. Eliot, introduction to *Inferno* by Dante Alighieri; https://futurestartup.com/2012/06/29/quotable-hell-is-a-place-where-nothing-connects-with-nothing/.

2. Ram Dass and Paul Gorman, chapter title in *How Can I Help? Stories and Reflections on Service* (New York: Alfred Knopf, 1985); https://aimhappy.com/walking-home-an-inspiring-poem/.

3. Maya Angelou; https://www.brainyquote.com/quotes/maya_angelou_392897.

4. "The Healing Power of Forgiveness," Johns Hopkins Health (Summer 2014), 7–10, Hopkinsmedicine.org/usa.

5. Fritz Perls; https://www.optimize.me/quotes/fritz-perls/21744-fear-is-excitement-without-the-breath/. Also attributed to businessman Robert Heller; https://www.goodreads.com/quotes/46600-fear-is-excitement-without-breath.

6. Leonard Cohen, "Anthem": https://www.azlyrics.com/lyrics/leonardcohen/anthem.html.

7. Rilke; https://quotefancy.com/quote/892854/Rainer-Maria-Rilke-Love-and-death-are-the-great-gifts-that-are-given-to-us-mostly-they.

8. Rumi; http://www.thewisdompost.com/self-improvement/thought/seek-seeking-rumi/2611.

ABOUT THE AUTHOR

Dani McGuire is a yoga therapist, yoga teacher, and ayurveda wellness counselor. She is the founder of Pranayoga Institute of Yoga and Holistic Health in Fort Wayne, Indiana. In 2009, she founded the Pranayoga Foundation, a 501(c)(3) nonprofit dedicated to providing free adaptive yoga classes to people dealing with cancer, addiction, trauma, chronic illness, and pain management. Dani is also the creator of the Sattva Vinyasa™ method, a style of regenerative flow influenced by vinyasa, yoga therapy, and Ayurveda. Dani's Sattva Therapy™ Yoga Therapy Diploma Program is among the first twenty-five programs worldwide to be accredited by the International Association of Yoga Therapists. Dani's fluency in the many languages of yoga allows her to meet students where they are, blending the Eastern philosophies of yoga, tantra, and ayurveda with modern living.

Dani began practicing yoga in 1995 and has been a yoga therapist since 2007. She has developed several

DVDs featuring Sattva Vinyasa and specialty practices for pregnancy and adaptive yoga for cancer. A full library of online practices is available at www.sattvavinyasa.com. Dani leads teacher trainings and workshops at Pranayoga Institute and around the world.

For more information about Dani and her work, visit www.sattvavinyasa.com.

You can also connect with her on social media:

Facebook
www.facebook.com/pranayogainstitute

Instagram
@pranayogainstitute
@sattvavinyasa

Made in the
USA
Columbia, SC